CEDED AT DAWN

Ceded at Dawn

The Aborted Decolonization of the UN Trust Territory of British Southern Cameroons

Augustine Ndangam

Spears Media Press
Denver, Colorado

Spears Media Press LLC
DENVER
7830 W. Alameda Ave, Suite 103-247 Denver, CO 80226
United States of America

First Published in 2020 by Spears Media Press
www.spearsmedia.com
info@spearsmedia.com
Information on this title: www.spearsmedia.com/ceded-at-dawn

© 2020 Augustine Ndangam

Library of Congress Control Number: 2020933761

ISBN: 9781942876526 (Paperback)
ISBN: 9781942876533 (eBook)

Typeset by Spears Media Press in 10.5/13pt Georgia

Dedicated to Gilbert, Julius and Clarence
And to their elder sister
Ma Marie Tita, star of the family
All of whom tided me over

"There can be no justification of injustice"

His Excellency, the High Commissioner of the British Southern Cameroon, Sir James Robertson in his farewell address to the people of the British Southern Cameroons on Wednesday 13th September 1961 in Buea. Published by the Government Press Buea in House of Assembly Debates (Official Report).

Contents

Illustrations

FIGURES

TABLES

FOREWORD

Browsing through Augustine Ndangam's enigmatic essay title, "Ceded at Dawn," what immediately hit me were memories of the iconic Reith Lectures broadcast over BBC Radio 4. Reflection and further in-depth reading of the essay only confirmed my initial gut feeling. The Reith Lectures are a series of annual lectures delivered by leading world figures of the day inaugurated in 1948. Clearly, Ndangam's treatise falls within than unique category and can best be understood not in isolation but within such a context, where, juxtaposed with his literary ilk, his profile and that of his work stand out more clearly. Though all comparisons are lame, because no two situations can be identical, the full weight of the essay can be projected that way. *Ceded at Dawn* is a world class production following standard norms.

Within that context, the voice that resonated loud and clear in my mind's eye, was that of Wole Soyinka, the 1986 Nobel Prize Laureate; playwright, poet, novelist and political activist with whom Augustine Ndangam shares a common platform in several traits even in the resonance of their voices. This emerges in Wole Soyinka's fifth and final Reith Lecture: "I am right; you are dead," Climate of Fear: 2004.

Remarkably, both men are literary luminaries under diverse circumstances. However, in this discourse, Ndangam shares Soyinka's legendary approach and audacity in maintaining that: "The man dies in all who keep silent in the face of tyranny" and that, "The greatest threat to freedom is the absence of criticism". These themes run powerfully throughout Ndangam's fascinating erudite essay written from concrete experience, displaying wisdom, knowledge and maturity. Mutually, they are intellectuals of class, audacious, seasoned pedagogues and political activists, who have tasted life behind bars, 'Prison Graduates' so to speak! Both men are retirees and belong to the same age grade; the difference being that Soyinka is an emeritus university don enjoying international academic repute, while the other is no less an intellectual, imbued with uncommon oratorical skills, wit and charm perfected by a sound academic formation and mellowed by decades of distinguished contributions to educational administration, community leadership and teaching of literature. The differences therefore are a function of opportunity, place and time but the duo would certainly recognize themselves and their talents if they were chanced to encounter each other.

Ndangam's work is a highly compacted confluence of factual, historical, legal, philosophical, sociological and archival sources enriched with copious lately bewildering, scandalous, incriminating, highly confidential and secret British documents. Ndangam has painstakingly analysed, logically parcelled out and put together with zeal, conviction and passion, spiced with rick literary anecdotes with unflinching faith and hope, confident with divine justice the truth shall prevail.

The essay meticulously highlights the flaws in the entire process of decolonization in the Southern Cameroons, unveils the masquerades contrived by Great Britain as the Mandatory Power and even worse as the Trusteeship Authority over the territory. It unveils the inconceivable collusion between Great Britain and the United Nations, organising an irrelevant, inconsequential plebiscite in the territory as a cover up, the results of which they totally failed to implement as all along they had conspired to stultify the independence of Southern Cameroons. The worst of the crimes against Southern Cameroons was the non-execution of the Resolution 1608 XV in which the Republic of Cameroon voted against the independence of Southern Cameroons but which finally had it thrust upon her. The abandonment of Southern Cameroons in the rapacious hands of the Republic of Cameroon, over time literally led to its brutal annexation by the Republic of Cameroon. Ndangam's greatest contribution is in establishing the fact that ultimately nothing binds the two former German colonies together and all that is required is legally retracing the illegal steps leading to its annexation and liberating the independent state of Southern Cameroons. In one word, executing the retarded process of "RESTORATION".

However, it must be cautioned that although highly distilled and simplified, the essay nevertheless remains an intriguing academic exposition not to be browsed through hurriedly, nor is it destined for the lightheaded. It may therefore be advisable to read it carefully, if not repeatedly to elicit its intrinsic goal. Finally, the facts and objectivity marshalled out of this essay should leave few people in doubt but like with all intellectual pursuits and, given the controversial nature of the topic, conscious of turbulent times the country is experiencing, the views and conclusions reached certainly would differ, but the intellectual solidity of the work incontestably stands.

Anthony Ndi, PhD, SOAS London
Associate Professor of History, CATUC, Bamenda

INTRODUCTION

This essay is about Southern Cameroons. The essay looks at how the country was surrendered at the moment of its attainment of independence from colonial rule, and how the mistaken dawn for the people of the territory turned into a nightmare of carnage. It sets out to make a sober assessment of the injustice that was done to the people and territory of the British Southern Cameroons in the process of an aborted decolonization that extinguished British Southern Cameroons from existence and abandoned the people and territory in an orbit of imminent catastrophe that could have been avoided by following the road-map for decolonization laid out in the UN Charter and the Trusteeship Agreement. In a second essay (*Massacre in the Gulf of Guinea*) the author continues with the theme of injustice. The root cause of the genocide in British Southern Cameroons was a combination of ignoring the agreement between the parties concerned, bypassing the key United Nations Resolutions and unlawfully transferring the British Southern Cameroons to French Cameroon on no known terms.

The invasion of (and genocide in) British Southern Cameroons has shocked the world. As a United Nations' Trust Territory with a self-governing status, a Ministerial government, a bicameral Legislature, and a Special Representative at the United Nations it comes as a surprise to many that the decolonization of British Southern Cameroons ended up with the territory being surrendered, annexed and split into two provinces of a neighbouring state, and re-colonized.

The story of mankind on this planet shows that the strongest force that has shaped human history is man's innate desire to be free. Throughout human history people have fought wars in order to live their own lives as they choose, not as someone else decides for them. Human beings have fought in order to break the chains that enslaved them. The war in Cameroon declared by President Biya is one such wars: a fight for freedom. The surprise about the war is that it is the colonial ruler (French Cameroon) that attacked and British Southern Cameroons (BSC) is on the defense. French Cameroon decided to take up arms to enforce annexation and the assimilation of BSC into a "one and indivisible Cameroon". On their part, the people of BSC regard the invasion and the excuses given for it as flimsy and baseless. There is world-wide acceptance that the Boko haram insurgency in Northern Cameroon has manifested itself as terrorism but there has been no report of terrorism activity in English speaking Southern Cameroons. The other excuse that part of Cameroon is seceding is also an untenable pretext for carrying out genocide on a people and territory you claim (but cannot defend or prove) in court that they are a part of your country. Thus, the people of BSC see the attack as an existential threat to the people of BSC who are determined to fight to the last man. They have no trained army but they are determined to deny French Cameroon the glory of victory. With the exception of Ethiopia and Liberia that were never colonized many African countries fought similar wars with colonial masters in order to be free from colonial rule. BSC too must be free. For a people to be free they must be citizens of a free political community. A free political community is that in which one is not ruled by foreigners or coerced into doing what they do not want to do. Such a community is self-governing, and its citizens play a direct and active role in the government of the community making laws that reflect the wishes and acceptance of the people. Such is the aspiration of the people of the former British Southern Cameroons. Such was the aspiration of most African countries prior to the event of decolonization.

It is in fact, much more than an aspiration. Self -determination is an inalienable right enshrined in the UN Charter. What follows in this essay therefore is an analysis on how the decolonization of the British Southern Cameroons ended not with the independence of the territory but with British Cameroons ceded, annexed, extinguished and obliterated.

The British Southern Cameroons was prior to 1961 the southern half of British Cameroons - a strip of territory in the Gulf of Guinea covering 16,581 square miles. Like other African countries, British Southern Cameroons experienced colonial rule and an extended post-colonial rule under Republic of Cameroon. It is the story of a prolonged colonial rule on the continent of Africa. Both British Cameroons and the Republic of Cameroon (former French Cameroon) had in 1884 formed part of a German colony which came to be divided between Britain and France at the end of World War I.

After the First World War, both British Cameroons and French Cameroun became League of Nations Mandates (1922-1945) and after 1945 the Mandated Territories were placed under the International Trusteeship System (ITS) of the United Nations. As set out in chapter XII and XIII of the UN Charter the ITS dealt with the supervision of the non-self-governing states designated as Trust Territories.

Trust Territories were to be placed under the ITS by separate agreements with the administering authorities like the United Kingdom in the case of British Cameroon. Although this essay is about British Southern Cameroon it is necessary to point out here that the British Cameroons comprised, Southern and Northern Cameroons separated by a 72 km (45 miles) strip along the River Benue.

The basic objective of the ITS as declared in Article 76 of the UN Charter was the promotion of the political, economic, social and educational advancement of the inhabitants of the Trust Territories and their progressive development towards self -government or independence. British Cameroon which had been administered under the League of Nations Mandate thus became a Trust Territory of the UN with a Trusteeship Agreement approved on 13 December 1946.

In September 1961 the British High Commissioner of the Southern Cameroons Sir James Robertson was in Buea to bid farewell to the people of the Southern Cameroons on behalf of Her Majesty's government. In his farewell speech delivered in the Southern Cameroons House of Assembly he used the occasion to comment on British administration in Southern Cameroons during 40 years of administration. Sir James Robertson said correctly that what had been done or left undone in Southern Cameroons was written on the pages of history for all to see.

However, on that same occasion, Sir James Robertson, Governor General of Nigeria addressing the Southern Cameroons in his capacity as High Commissioner used seven words which ironically were to boomerang on the British administration after that event to become the scale balance on which British Administration in Cameroon was to be assessed by history. Those seven words spoken at 10AM on Wednesday 13th September 1961 were "There can be no justification of injustice."

The purpose of this essay is to show by analysis how the people of the United Nation's Trust Territory of the British Southern Cameroons became victims of a failed decolonization process and how their country was ceded, annexed and recolonized in the process of decolonization. The reader is free to agree with Sir James Robertson that he was not in Buea to justify injustice or with the present writer that grave injustice was done to the people of British Southern Cameroons.

However, if we are going to see the world as a just and fair place where everyone is given equal opportunities and if the United Nations is going to "Sav-e succeeding generations from the scourge of war and foster fundamental human rights and the equal rights of men and women of nations large and small and develop friendly relations among nations based on respect for the principle of equal rights and self-determination of peoples," (UN Charter) then what happened to British Southern

Cameroons in the process of decolonization should never happen again anywhere in the world in a process initiated, funded and supervised by the United Nations.

PART I

❧

IN THE NAME OF DECOLONIZATION

Chapter 1

BRITISH CAMEROONS IS DISMEMBERED

Prior to the event of independence for colonial countries in Africa, British West Africa comprised (West to East) of: The Gambia, Sierra Leone, Ghana, British Togoland, Nigeria and the British Cameroons. British Togoland and British Cameroons were United Nations Trust Territories administered by the United Kingdom. Both countries had earlier been League of Nations' Mandates from 1922 to the outbreak of WWII. British Cameroons and French Cameroons once made up the German colony of Kamerun (1884 – 1914). Germany lost all its colonies at the end of WW I and Kamerun came to be divided between the United Kingdom and France at the Versailles Peace Conference and a Mandate system established (Appendix 1).

The British took advantage of Article 9 of its mandate that "the Mandatory shall have full powers of administration and legislation in the area subject to the mandate. This area shall be administered in accordance with the laws of the Mandatory as an integral part of his territory" to administer British Cameroons as part of Nigeria and for that purpose to divide the territory into two: Northern Cameroons attached to Northern Nigeria and Southern Cameroons attached to Eastern Nigeria. In this position, Southern Cameroons formed part of the British Empire and later part of the British Commonwealth.

At the end of WW II, the United Nations replaced the League of Nations and the International Trusteeship System of the United Nations (ITS) was established in Chapter XII (Articles 75-85) of the Charter and the Trusteeship Council in Chapter XIII (Articles 86-91) to monitor Trust Territories. Individual Trust Territories were subject to separate trusteeship agreements with the administering states, because they were formally administered under Mandates from the League of Nations or were separated from countries defeated in the Second World War or were voluntarily placed under the system by States responsible for their administration. Eleven Territories including the British Cameroons were placed under this system.

The decision by the United Kingdom to administer British Cameroons as part of Nigeria was said to be "for administrative convenience." Elsewhere in West Africa, British Togoland was also administered as part of the neighbouring British colony of the Gold Coast.

TABLE 1.1: UN Trust Territories and Self–determination

Trust Territory	Administration	Form of Self-determination
Togoland	British	United with Gold Coast to form Ghana
Somaliland	Italian	United with British Somaliland to form Somalia
Togoland	French	Became independent as Togo (1960)
Cameroon	French	Became independent as Cameroon (1960)
Cameroon	British	Northern Cameroons joined Nigeria (1 June 1961) Southern Cameroons joined Republic of Cameroon (1 October 1961
Tanganyika	British	Became independent 1961. United with Zanzibar in 1964 to form the United Republic of Tanzania
Ruanda - Urundi	Belgian	Voted to separate into two Sovereign States of Rwanda and Burundi (1962)
Western Samoa	New Zealand	Became independent as Samoa (1962)
Nauru	Australia on behalf of Australia, New Zealand and the UK	Became independent 1968
New Guinea	Australia	United with Papua to form Papua New Guinea in 1975

Trust Territory of the Pacific Island		Free Association with the United States (1990)
Federated State of Micronesia		Free Association with the United States (1990)
Republic of the Marshall Island	The United States	Free Association with the United States (1990)
Commonwealth of the Northern Mariana Islands		Commonwealth of the United States (1990)
Palau		Free Association with the United States (1994)

As shown on the table above, French Cameroon became independent as Cameroon on January 1, 1960. On this date BSC was still a UN Trust Territory.

All the British colonies in West Africa including the UN Trust territories under British administration went through the same (British) colonial experience. In all of them, English language was the official language and the medium of instruction in schools. In all of them British education aimed at modernizing the African culture. In the primary and secondary schools, the content of the curricula was similar and schools in these countries used common text books in many of the subjects on the curriculum and wrote common secondary school certificate examinations set from the United Kingdom. These countries inherited the same judicial system and common law practice and in commercial activities major British banks like Barclays and the Bank of British West Africa operated in all these countries using the West Africa pounds and shillings.

Then came the event of decolonization at the end of World War II. Under chapter XI (Articles 73 and 74) the Charter of the United Nations had established the principles to guide the UN decolonization including respect for self-determination of all peoples.

The Gold Coast became independent as Ghana in 1957, Nigeria in 1960, Sierra Leone in 1961 and the Gambia in 1965. All the four British colonies in West Africa gained full independence and became sovereign states. Before Ghana achieved its independence, British Togoland was asked in a plebiscite to choose between becoming independent by remaining as part of Ghana or waiting for separate independence afterwards. They chose immediate independence as part of Ghana. For the British Cameroons the full consequence of dismemberment was to surface with the territory's own decolonization. For denying both Northern Cameroons and Southern Cameroons full independence the

3

United Kingdom as Administering Authority put forward the idea that each of these two territories was too small and too poor to accede to sovereign independence. If the Administering Authority believed that dividing British Cameroons into two and attaching each half to different parts of Nigeria would diminish both halves and disqualify them for independence why did they divide the territory in the first place? That apart, what demographic criteria was there for Trust Territory to attain in order to qualify for sovereign independence?

The other idea hatched by the Administering Authority to deny the people of British Cameroons their independence was that the territory was poor. When this excuse was put forward (and in so far as the Southern Cameroons was concerned) it was forgotten that only ten years earlier (for the financial year 1949 - 1950) the Southern Cameroons revenue had reached £1,053,240 exceeding its expenditure and leaving a surplus of £310,280. It is difficult to see how a territory's revenue could exceed expenditure leaving a surplus and the territory came to be "too poor" to be independent shortly afterwards.

In a letter to the chiefs of Mambila on the 5th of August 1960, John Ngu Foncha, Prime Minister of the Southern Cameroons in his capacity as KNDP President General wrote:

> The British have divided us into two parts and are doing everything possible to see that we do not meet but we all Northern and Southern Cameroons know that we are brothers and are trying to bring ourselves together into one country.

Although the British claimed all along that the attachment of parts of British Cameroons to Nigeria was for administrative convenience, Her Majesty's Government nursed private plans to finally incorporate the territory into Nigeria making this to look like a decision of the people themselves. The event of Nigeria's independence brought the question of what happens to the fragmented Trust Territory of British Cameroons. To the East French Cameroon had acceded to sovereign independence on January 1, 1960 and the UK accelerated plans to incorporate British Cameroons into Nigeria. Under both the Mandate and Trusteeship British Cameroon had been a single territory. The Council of the League of Nations had not conferred separate mandates for Northern Cameroon and Southern Cameroons in 1922, and the United Nations had not signed separate TrusteeshipAgreements for each part of the dismembered Territory.

At the UN, Britain was repeatedly giving assurances of preserving the

Territory as a single entity until it achieved independence in accordance with the terms of the Trusteeship Agreement. In the UN Trusteeship Council meeting held at the Palaise des Nations, Geneva on 7 March 1950 to examine the annual reports on the administration of Trust Territories, the British excuses for dividing British Cameroons into two began to emerge: Why did the United Kingdom delegate its responsibility for the Trust Territory to the colonial government of Nigeria? Was this not a violation of the Trusteeship Agreement and a breach of the faith reposed by the United Nations in the Administering Authority that they were responsible for the conditions prevailing in the Territory? Whether or not there was any sense of unity developing among the people of the Northern and Southern Cameroons and what steps the Administering Authority was taking to promote political development towards self-government or independence?

The representative of the Administering Authority at the meeting evaded the first question but went on to say that in Northern Cameroons there was a complete lack of cohesion in the territory owing to the physical distances separating the lands in which the people lived as in Dikwa and Adamawa. In the South on the other hand, although a great diversity of people existed, unity was easier and could be developed. The Administering Authority cited the example of the emergence of the Cameroon National Federation formed by the educated elements in the South. Brigadier Gibbons from the territory itself insisted on what the Administering Authority was complaining about that between the North and the South of British Cameroons, there was no feeling of a common identity. Indeed, the Administering Authority suggested that in their view, social division ran East-West not North-South. This was already the thinking preparatory to the merger of the Northern Cameroons with Northern Nigeria instead of with Southern part of British Cameroons. The lack of North-South cohesion in British Cameroons and the difficulty expressed in fostering them were all administrative excuses and tactics. The British were deliberately working to minimize North-South links within the territory while facilitating East-West ones with Nigeria. This can be seen from the fact that outside the territory itself the French had no difficulty fostering cohesion between North and South in French Cameroon. In Nigeria itself the British had no problem with North-South cohesion prior to Nigeria's independence as they alleged in British Cameroons where they claimed that for natural and ethical reasons it was impossible to develop the whole Trust Territory into a single political entity. This situation according to the British did not mean that the territory was being given a different treatment from what it would have received if it were a part of Nigeria. The policy of the Administering Authority was to raise the Trust Territory to the same high level as that of Nigeria and eventually lead it to self-government.

According to Sir Alan Burns (UK representative), Britain was determined to preserve the Trust Territory as a separate entity in accordance with the terms of the Trusteeship Agreement and lead it to self-government in the same manner as other colonies under British administration. That was "definitely a matter, not of words, but of fact."

While saying all these to the United Nations, Britain in the same breath was taking advantage of their administration of British Cameroons under the Mandate and kept echoing on some other problems of the territory which proceeded the birth of the United Nations. By reason of integration during the time of the mandate it had become impossible to "unscramble" the parts of the territory and the natural development of various segments tended to take place on east-west rather than north-south lines. With excuses like this Britain, was quietly working to divide the territory and incorporate the Northern section to Northern Nigeria in a manner as to give the impression that such a development arose entirely from the wishes of the people.

Soon the excuse was to give way to the language of justification when it was clear that Northern Cameroons and Southern Cameroons were separate entities. Brigadier Gibbons now asserted at the UN that there was a distinction between the Southern part of British Cameroons and the Northern part: The Southern part had retained their individuality and had not been subject to complete integration. The Northern half on the other hand had not formed a natural entity but was part of social units which were centred outside the Trust Territory (alluding to Northern Nigeria). That state of affairs had not been created by the Administering Authority but had existed when it assumed the trusteeship.

The Road Map is Changed

By road map in this section we mean two things:
a). The objectives of the International Trusteeship System which are set out in Chapter XII of the UN Charter and
b). The undertakings by the Administering Authority in the Trusteeship Agreement signed on 13 December 1946.

These two documents are clear that the objectives of the UN Trusteeship were self-government or independence and the undertaking by the administering Authority was to work to achieve these objectives. We need to pause here and look closely at the motivating circumstances by which the procedures set out in the charter and the Trusteeship Agreement came to be set aside and a controversial plebiscite conducted.

The meeting of the UN General Assembly of 21st April 1961 adopted several resolutions on a wide range of subjects including that on the dissemination of information (1607) and the one on the future of Tanganyika (1609 XV). The need to disseminate information to the people of the Trust Territories concerning the purpose and operation of the United Nations and of the International Trusteeship system, the principle of the Universal Declaration of Human Rights and the Declaration of the granting of independence to colonial countries and peoples, UN (GA) Resolution 1514 XV of 14th December 1960, were belated though necessary.

By Resolution 1607 XV, the Secretary General of the UN was directed to ensure "The immediate and mass publication and the widest possible circulation and dissemination in all Trust Territories through all media of mass communication of the Declaration on the granting of independence to colonial countries and people." This was clearly an important directive, but it was also (as far as the British Cameroons was concerned) medication after death. The fate of Southern Cameroons had already been sealed (Resolution 1608 XV).

Three separate Plebiscites (two in Northern Cameroons and one in Southern Cameroons) had already been concluded concerning the independence of these territories and the very next item on the agenda of the General Assembly for that day was for the UN to formally endorse the outcome of these plebiscites and set the dates for terminating the Trusteeship Agreement for the two territories. Thus, the first controversy about the UN Plebiscite in the British Southern Cameroons on 11th February 1961 is that it was being conducted without preparing the people of British Southern Cameroons enough on the content of the UN Resolution 1607 XV, which was adopted on the same day as Resolution 1608 XV (Appendix 4). The others relate to the violation of the charter itself. We will take up later. Here, let's go back one year earlier (1960) and glance at the categories of independence set up by the United Nations.

Different Categories of Independence

The decolonization process in British Southern Cameroons shows clearly that the adoption in 1960 of UN Resolution 1541 XV defining *free association* with an *independent State*, Integration into an independent state and independence as the three options offering "full self-government" did nothing other than help advance and assist colonial interest at the detriment of the inhabitants of the Trust Territories.

If we place the three categories of self-government in order of attractiveness (the UN does not), we may have something like this:

A. Independence
B. Free association with an independent state
C. Integration into an independent state.

What is meant by "full" in the concept of "full self-government" remains unclear. If this "full" means "complete" it would imply that no matter which category of independence a Territory got, all should be admitted into membership of the UN. The UN Trust Territory of French Cameroon got category A independence on 1st January 1960. The UN flag was lowered in Yaoundé in the presence of the Secretary General of the UN, and the Republic of Cameroon was admitted as a member of the UN on 20th September 1960. British Cameroons on the other hand had category B independence on 1st October 1961. The UN flag was never lowered, and the territory was never recommended for UN membership, yet both are said to have achieved "full self- government"? The UN flag was officially handed to British Cameroons by the UN visiting Mission in 1949. At midnight on September 30th, 1961 this flag was never lowered to mark the end of UN Trusteeship in Southern Cameroons and the blue and white stripes of the British Southern Cameroons flag raised to mark Southern Cameroons attainment of "full" self-government. Can it therefore be said that British Southern Cameroons achieved "full" independence?

Inconsistencies and Violations of the Charter

The UN signed individual Trusteeship Agreements with the different administering Authorities. The key term common in all the Agreements was the undertaking by the different Administering Authorities to administer the territories in view of achieving Charter goals and the objectives of the Trusteeship System laid down in Article 76 of the Charter and provide for the defense of the Territory. At the termination of Trusteeship in some Territories the Trusteeship Agreement was set aside and a plebiscite used while others had their own self-government in accordance with the Trusteeship Agreement. The plebiscite in British Southern Cameroons was a major violation of the UN Charter and the terms of the Trusteeship Agreement. The plebiscite introduced conditional independence for British Southern Cameroons. As a matter of fact, the plebiscite came as a means of preventing independence for British Southern Cameroons. More than that, what the plebiscite accomplished was to extinguish British Southern Cameroons together with its self-governing status.

Before the plebiscite, Foncha (Prime Minister of Southern Cameroons) and Ahidjo of the Republic of Cameroon had earlier agreed to create a federation of two States called the Federal United Cameroon Republic and that the two States in the federation were to have equal status. Given the fact that these points of agreement were available to both the Administering Authority and the UN, the inconsistency between paragraphs 4a and 4b of Resolution 1608 XV (Appendix 4) comes as a surprise: In 4a the status of Northern Cameroons when it joined Nigeria is stated, in 4b the status of the self-governing Southern Cameroons when it joined the Republic of Cameroon is not stated.

What emerges at the end of the series of inconsistencies and violations is that a crack is found which opens up an unexpected opportunity for Republic of Cameroon who knew all along that the plebiscite in BSC was for that territory joining either Nigeria or the Republic of Cameroon but decided when the chips were down to take an embarrassing position by voting against BSC joining Republic of Cameroon, a vote which cornered the United Nations and vetoed the proposal for BSC joining Republic of Cameroon. The UK solution to the dilemma was to cede Southern Cameroons to Republic of Cameroon and permanently shelve Resolution 1608 XV which in the circumstance was not enforceable. The Republic of Cameroon registered its objection to Southern Cameroons joining her. On the other hand, now that it had come down to ceding the territory, Republic of Cameroon was prepared to annex Southern Cameroons on her own terms but not as equals.

"Independence by Joining" is Conceived

When the word "independence" has been applied to states or nations it always has been understood as independence from foreign rule. The word has historically been understood as freedom of the people and this understanding regards independence as something beneficiary to the people concerned. However, as mentioned above, under Resolution 1541 (XV) of 15 December 1960 the UN recognized three kinds of independence. "Independence by joining" was never an option when the International Trusteeship System was established and certainly did not feature anywhere in the Trusteeship Agreement.

"Independence by Joining" suppressed the independence of British Southern Cameroons, subverted the agreement on "States of Equal status" and subordinated British Southern Cameroons to French Cameroon all of which served only the colonial interest of the outgoing and the incoming colonial rulers at the detriment of the people of Southern Cameroons and their future. Some may argue that it was the people of Southern Cameroons themselves who made their choice to join the Republic of Cameroon. This of course, is untenable. Southern Cameroons did not ask for a plebiscite and when for some flimsy excuse this was forced down their throat, the 3rd choice was ruled out against the people's wishes. Thus, the UN plebiscite with its experiment on "independence by joining" was the first step in sending Southern Cameroons to be annexed. It violated the UN Charter and breached the Trusteeship Agreement. The UK campaigned vigorously at the UN to the effect that the Southern Cameroons was too small and poor to be a sovereign nation. Yet many sovereign countries that are members of the Commonwealth are smaller than Southern Cameroons.

Size apart, was the Southern Cameroons poor? Indeed, Southern Cameroons was thought to be poor and any superficial economic study that reached this conclusion justified "independence by joining" but time was to reveal a different fact. For decades following the ceding of the Territory, it was the natural resources of the Southern Cameroons that was being raped and carted off for the exclusive development of the new colonial master that had replaced the UK in Southern Cameroon. During this period oil revenue from the National Refining Company (SONARA) located in Southern Cameroons never featured on the national budget. Annual production figures remained a guarded secret known only by the President (a Francophone) and the Director of SONARA became a position permanently reserved for Francophone appointees. Although SONARA is located in Victoria (English speaking) its taxes were paid to the Douala Municipality (on the French speaking side).

Implementing "independence by joining" after the plebiscite was not going to be an easy task. The Administering Authority had to bring clarity to ambiguities and look into legal implications of the UN statement. In the Plebiscite, the people of Southern Cameroons had been asked to achieve independence by joining either the Federation of Nigeria or the Federal Republic of Cameroon.

> If at midnight the sovereignty of the Southern Cameroons is transmitted to the Republic of Cameroon the people of the Southern Cameroons do not at that moment achieve independence. They lose their identity and become subjects of the Republic of Cameroon. It may well be that within a matter of minutes, hours or days the Republic will by an act of state transform itself into a federation of two states composed of the former Republic of Cameroons. The Southern Cameroons will then have achieved independence not by joining the Republic

of Cameroon but after joining the Republic of Cameroon. In order that the people of the Southern Cameroons may achieve independence by joining the Republic of Cameroon it is necessary that the Federation should come into existence at midnight of 1st October. At one and the same moment there will be born the independent state of the Southern Cameroons and the Federation of the United Kamerun Republic. The Federation would be a free association of independent and equal sovereign states (*British Declassified files*).

The idea of "independence by joining" in the UN Plebiscite in British Southern Cameroons was strikingly ridiculous and illogical. How was a self-governing territory going to achieve independence by choosing to give up their self-governing status and becoming a permanent dependency of another country already enjoying independence? Practically how was the administering authority going to implement this new international concept and be seen to have discharged her undertaking in the charter and the trusteeship agreement?

Her Majesty's government considered that if by midnight on the appointed date (1st October 1961) the sovereignty of the Southern Cameroons was transmitted to the Republic of Cameroon, then the people of Southern Cameroon were not achieving independence but losing their identity by becoming the subjects of the Republic of Cameroon. On the other hand, if the Republic of Cameroon within a short time (of hours or days) adopted an act of state transforming itself into a federation of two states (former Republic of Cameroon and Southern Cameroon) then Southern Cameroon would have achieved independence not by joining the Republic of Cameroon but after joining the Republic of Cameroon. To accomplish the UN "independence by joining," her Majesty's government was therefore of the view that the federation proposed in the plebiscite should come into existence at midnight on 1st October 1961. In that way there would be born the independent state of Southern Cameroons and the Federation of the United Kamerun Republic. The federation would be a free association of independent and equal sovereign states.

Before the plebiscite itself took place and following Resolution 2013 (XXVI) of the United Nations Trusteeship Council, the United Kingdom had obtained from the government of the Republic of Cameroon information regarding the constitutional arrangements to be made in the event of Southern Cameroons opting to join the Republic of Cameroon and the position agreed by the Republic of Cameroon appears in *The Two Alternatives* (the official document on the 1961 UN Plebiscite in

Southern Cameroons) as a Joint Communiqué by the Prime Minister of the Southern Cameroons and the President of the Republic of Cameroon.

This joint communiqué expressed mutual agreement with the interpretation of the second plebiscite question (joining the Republic of Cameroon), which interpretation had been made by the United Kingdom Secretary of State and proposed inter-alia that Southern Cameroons and the Republic of Cameroon would unite (on a date to be decided by the United Nations) in a Federal United Cameroon Republic. A key stipulation of the communiqué was the transfer of sovereign powers to an organization representing the future Federation. Her Majesty's government also argued that the UN plebiscite in Southern Cameroons had to be considered in its entirety. It was not possible to consider the two questions posed at the plebiscite in isolation.

> The people of the Southern Cameroons accepted joining the Republic of Cameroun after considering the constitutional offers which the Republic made in the two communiqués. Those communiqués have become the terms of a constitutional contract which the Republic of Cameroun is obliged to honour and has agreed to honour. It is submitted that it is clear beyond peradventure that the Republic of Cameroun has contracted to receive the Southern Cameroons as an equal sovereign state and at one and the same time to form with it a federation of two equal sovereign states (*British declassified files*).

On its part Nigeria had undertaken to welcome British Southern Cameroons as part of the Federation with the status of a full self- governing region equal in all respects with the other Regions in an independent Nigeria. At the time Nigeria had 3 Regions: the Northern, Eastern and Western Regions. Southern Cameroons (if it chose to join Nigeria) was going to become the fourth Region. The undertaking by the Republic of Cameroon to welcome Southern Cameroons as an equal sovereign state was a more attractive choice to the Southern Cameroons electorate. The implementation of this mutually agreed arrangement for the Federal United Cameroon Republic was to be worked out carefully with the participation of the Administering Authority and the UN: in particular how and to whom the sovereignty of the Southern Cameroons was to be transferred.

The Republic of Cameroun has agreed in the second communiqué that sovereign powers shall be transferred to an organization representing the future Federation. Since the State of the Southern Cameroon will be a sovereign, independent state equal in all respects to the Republic it is necessary that the organization of equal elements representing the Republic of the Cameroun and the State of the Southern Cameroons. It is not compatible with the dignity of the Southern Cameroons that, that organization should be the President of the Republic acting in association with the Head of State of the Southern Cameroons. It may be practicable to transfer sovereignty to the President of the Republic and the Head of the State of the Southern Cameroons jointly but it is submitted that the better course would be that proposed by the premier and Ministers of the Southern Cameroons namely a body composed of equal numbers of representatives nominated by the Government of the Southern Cameroons representatively, which body shall appoint a temporary president of the Federation. Sovereignty should only be transferred to an organization representing equally the Republic of Cameroon and the State of Southern Cameroons (*British declassified files*).

Her Majesty's government also noted that the Republic of Cameroon had agreed in the second communique that the sovereign powers of the Southern Cameroons was to be transferred to an organization representing a future federation. Since the state of the Southern Cameroons was going to be a sovereign, independent state equal in all respects to the Republic, it was necessary that the organization of the equal elements represent the Republic of Cameroon and the state of Southern Cameroons. It was not compatible with the dignity of the Southern Cameroons that, the organization should be the President of the Republic acting in association with the Head of State of Southern Cameroons jointly but the better course was the one by the premier and ministers of Southern Cameroons namely a body comprising equal members of representatives nominated by the government of Southern Cameroons representatively which body was to appoint a temporary president of the federation. Sovereignty was to be transferred only to an organization representing equally the Republic of Cameroon and the State of Southern Cameroons. Although Her Majesty's government took this important and particular note, on 27th September the note by Her

Majesty's government transferring the UN Trust Territory of Southern Cameroons was addressed to President Ahidjo of Cameroon Republic.

The plebiscite in British Togoland was completely different from the one in British Southern Cameroons. At the General Assembly meeting of 15th December 1955, the Assembly decided by a vote of 42 to 7 with 11 abstentions that the United Kingdom as Administering Authority should organize a plebiscite in British Togoland. Togoland was asked in the plebiscite to choose between remaining permanently as part of the Gold Coast which was soon to become independent or remain as a UN trust territory hoping that at some future date they will reunite with French Togoland. The referendum in British Togoland was held on 9 May 1956 and the result was 63.9% for integration with Ghana and 36.1% for continuing UN Trusteeship. These choices were fair, and the majority voted to continue as part of the Gold Coast.

In the British Southern Cameroons plebiscite, Foncha had won the 1959 general elections on a policy of separation from Nigeria and Southern Cameroons had acquired self-governing status. In British Togoland the UK was under pressure to grant independence to the Gold Coast following Dr. Kwame Nkrumah's election victory in the parliamentary election of 1954. As with the Southern Cameroons, Togoland had been a German colony until World War I. Following the defeat of Germany in World War I Togoland had been split into two parts and divided between Britain and France. As with Cameroon, Britain had decided to administer British Togoland as part of the British colony of the Gold Coast.

The British Southern Cameroons on its part was a self-governing state expecting the termination of Trusteeship and granting of sovereign independence, but the plebiscite choices were offering them conditional independence which required them to relinquish their self-governing status and join one of the neighbouring independent states (Nigeria or French Cameroons). This had thrown the Southern Cameroons electorate into a dilemma. The then Fon of Bafut described the two alternatives in the Southern Cameroons plebiscite as death by drowning or death by conflagration. Time was to prove the natural ruler perfectly right. A combination of the annexation of the Southern Cameroons as two provinces of the Republic of Cameroon, the suppression of their form of democracy with dictatorship and iron rule has generated growing resentment throughout the Southern Cameroons and the situation is made worse by the policy of France.

The Red Line which Anglophones in Cameroon Must Never Cross

This is the official policy from the highest State office in France on the Anglophones in Cameroon. Its purpose is to ensure that no English-speaking person in Cameroon should ever aspire to the highest office in Cameroon. It states clearly that should the people of Cameroon dare to vote John Fru Ndi (or any other Southern Cameroonian) France would intervene and use arms to put a Francophone in place. In other words, by this French Policy no English-speaking person in Cameroon can/ should ever hope to be President of Cameroon.

This policy statement by France aims at preventing any English-speaking person in Cameroon from aspiring to the highest state office in Cameroon. It is France standing between the State of Southern Cameroons and her self-determination. It is France that led the Francophone countries in Africa at the United Nations to vote against the independence of the BSC and against BSC joining the Republic of Cameroon (French Cameroon). It is France that prevailed on the Republic of Cameroon to set aside the agreement on "Federation of States of equal Status" and pursue annexation and assimilation. France is clear on its policy against Anglophones in Cameroon and that policy is the worst colonial idea of holding a people in subjugation. If there is to be change in Cameroon from Paul Biya to someone else it cannot be an Anglophone but a Francophone like Maigari Bello Bouba. The statement is also clear that should the people of Cameroon dare to vote John Fru Ndi or any other Anglophone again, France would intervene with arms to put a Francophone of their choice in place. In other words, by this French policy no English-speaking person in Cameroon must never hope to be president in Cameroon. Indeed, the participation of the Social Democratic Front (SDF) in elections in Cameroon is regarded in Paris as an inadmissible interference by Southern Cameroons in France's sphere of influence in Africa. The only solution for Anglophones in Cameroon therefore is to separate and restore their own statehood and the independence granted them by the General Assembly of the United Nations on 21st April 1961.

Charles de Gaulle (1890-1970), French General and the architect of the Fifth French Republic is reputed to have claimed in a *Le Monde* newspaper interview that Southern Cameroons was "un petite cadeau de La Reine" (a little gift from the Queen) and this claim is corroborated by a more shocking claim by a Minister in Mr. Biya's government that they (the Biya's government) gave the same Queen the largest mammal in Africa as a pet to reciprocate. This largest African mammal (obviously an elephant) is in one of the British zoos, not in the gardens of Buckingham Palace. These claims of exchanging a self-governing UN

Trust Territory of over six million people with an animal for a royal pet is a stinking story but whatever mud the story carries should be on the roof of the Whitehall, not Buckingham Palace.

British Southern Cameroons is Obliterated and Extinguished

So far, we have seen that the goal of independence in the Charter (Article 76) and the emphasis on the interest of the inhabitants of the Trust Territories (Article 73) - in fact, the entire road map in the Charter and Trusteeship Agreement - were brushed aside in British Cameroons and the decolonization of that territory was to be taken via a controversial plebiscite.

It was easy to substitute the goal of independence stated in the charter with an absurd form of "independence by joining." It was easy to decide that this new experiment will be accomplished via a plebiscite. What was difficult was the choices to be put to the electorate. What to ask the people in the plebiscite took place against a background of change of government in Southern Cameroons. The Prime Minister, Dr. E.M. Endeley was defeated by Mr. John Ngu Foncha's Kamerun National Democratic Party (KNDP) and Mr Foncha, although supporting a future unification with the Republic of Cameroon wanted Southern Cameroons to first achieve sovereign independence before negotiating the terms of unification from a position of strength. Foncha stated this position at the Special Session of the United Nations which met from 20 February to 13 March 1959 to determine the questions to be put at the plebiscite: "I am mandated by the House of Assembly and the majority of the people of the Southern Cameroons to place the following before the UN General Assembly as what they want".

a. "That we want the separation of the Southern Cameroons from the Federation of Nigeria before the latter attains independence in 1960.

b. That the Southern Cameroons be constituted into a separate entity and continue for a short time under United Kingdom Trusteeship. The Trusteeship Agreement should be modified to allow the Southern Cameroons to be administered separately from Nigeria. During this interim period the Southern Cameroons will work towards complete independence."

On the other hand, Dr. E.M. Endeley wanted Southern Cameroons to achieve Independence within the Federation of Nigeria. A third group, the One Kamerun (OK) led by Mr. Ndeh Ntunmazah and made up of the remnants of the UPC after it was banned from Southern Cameroons in 1957, took up the banned UPC slogan, of *Immediate Unification.*

Faced with these three options, the United Nations requested the Administering Authority to summon a conference of all shades of political opinions in Southern Cameroons to determine the questions to be put at the impending UN plebiscite. This conference held in Mamfe and the KNDP, CPNC and OK parties maintained their positions stated above. By this time, two other parties had emerged: the Kamerun United Party (KUP), led by P.M. Kale and the Cameroons Commoner's Congress (CCC) led by Chief S.E. Nyenti. These two parties advocated separation from Nigeria and independence within the commonwealth. They had mustered support in Victoria and Mamfe and their views were spreading significantly throughout Southern Cameroons. It was obvious that these two new parties would win overwhelmingly in the plebiscite. They were expressing the true wishes of the people, but their views were not going to see the light of day. The regrettable thing that happened in all these was that in deciding what questions to put to the electorate the United Nations overlooked the position of the majority leader John Ngu Foncha and took the positions of the minority leader, Dr. E. M.L. Endeley and the other minority leader Ndeh Ntumazah. In finally deciding in this manner the United Nations violated a key democratic principle that the majority have its way while the minority have its say.

Decolonization is Aborted and Abandoned

Also, according to *The Two Alternatives of the 1961 Southern Cameroons Plebiscite* published before the plebiscite, the Southern Cameroons electorate were informed that the UN was going to be at the post-plebiscite conference. This promise had some effect on the choice by the people especially when by Report of the Trusteeship Council No A/C 4/L 685 of 18 April, the UN was reminded of that pre-plebiscite commitment to the Southern Cameroons electorate and urged to send three constitutional and administrative experts to Cameroon for the post-plebiscite conference but the UN never turned up and the post plebiscite conference itself never held. After adopting Resolution 1608 XV both the UN and the Administering Authority abandoned the plebiscite process midstream and backed out. The UK ceded the territory to the Republic of Cameroon on 27th September 1961 and the UN acquiesced. Nothing was heard of the United Nations in relation to the Trust Territory of the Southern Cameroons after the 21st of April 1961. The pre-plebiscite plan of a post-plebiscite conference at which both the UN and the Administering Authority were to attend was permanently consigned to oblivion.

The plebiscite process, indeed, the entire decolonization process in British Southern Cameroons came to be abandoned after the adoption of UN Resolution 1608 XV on April 21 1961. What was still to be done after that date?

1. The post-Plebiscite Conference promised in The Two Alternatives in the event that the vote of the plebiscite went in favour of joining the Republic of Cameroon and UN Commitment to attend that conference. The vote did go in favour of joining the Republic of Cameroon. In their final report No. A/C.4/L.685 of 18 April 1961 on The Question of the Future of the Cameroons under United Kingdom administration, the Trusteeship Council reminded the UN General Assembly (paragraph 6) of UN commitment to attend that Post Plebiscite Conference. The Trusteeship Council went further to propose that three Constitutional and administrative experts be appointed to represent the UN at the Conference. Yet that conference never held at all.

2. The Tripartite Conference set up in Resolution 1608 XV to make detail arrangements before October 1, 1961 for British Southern Cameroons joining the Republic of Cameroon had not executed that assignment and reported and there is no evidence that the Committee ever even sat. What was expected of that UN Committee was to draw up a Treaty of Union and write a Constitution for uniting the 2 States before the date of October 1, 1961. Given that the Republic of Cameroon had explicitly turned down the UN proposal for British Southern Cameroons joining her and this UN proposal was now being pushed, it was all the more imperative for the terms of the UN-proposed union to be formalized in a legal instrument signed by parties, ratified by their respective Parliaments and registered at the UN Secretariat. This was never done.

PART II

❦

HEADS I WIN, TAILS YOU LOSE

Chapter 2

PLEBISCITE ON INDEPENDENCE: A COSMETIC EXERCISE IN DEMOCRACY

The February 11th, 1961 UN plebiscite on independence in British Southern Cameroons has rightly been described as a "cosmetic exercise in democracy" by Mr. John Percival, television broadcaster and staff of the BBC who served in that UN plebiscite in Southern Cameroons as a Plebiscite Supervisory Officer. In his posthumous memoir edited by his wife Lalage Neal titled *The 1961 Cameroon Plebiscite: Choice or Betrayal,* John Percival states in the preface of the book:

> The sheer arrogance of this enterprise still takes my breath away. In no way was I, or anyone else qualified to impose such a process on thousands of people and it was quickly made clear to me they wanted no part of it and that they saw the whole thing as a sham, a cosmetic exercise in democracy. The only decision they were allowed to make was to choose whether to throw in their lot with Nigeria or French Cameroon and they wanted neither of them. All the other decisions had been taken thousands of miles away by officials who thought they knew what they needed better than the people themselves.

The reason why Mr. Percival's description of that event is apt and appropriate is that this was a plebiscite that purported to be about "independence" but it strikingly excluded the option of independence itself and the people of Southern Cameroons desperately called for this to be included but they were told that the UN had ruled out such an option.

In both the Charter and the Trusteeship Agreement the goal of self-government or independence are stated without pre-conditions. The question of the plebiscite introduced conditional independence:

    a.   Do you wish to achieve independence by joining the independent Federation of Nigeria?

    b.   Do you wish to achieve independence by joining the independent

Republic of Cameroon?

Which meant that independence for the people of Southern Cameroons was on condition that they joined another independent state.

Years later, in a critique of the British government's view that the creation of the Welsh Assembly whose members were nominated rather than elected was a way to democratise local governments whose members were elected locally, Ian Grist, (MP Cardiff North) argued in the British House of Parliament that such a position was a mockery to the democracy. He went on to cite another instance where the autonomy of a people was mocked.

> It reminds me that some years ago I served in a plebiscite in the southern Cameroons. We had to tell the people of that particular colony that they were to become independent by choosing to join one of their two large neighbours. That was the way in which this little group of people became independent. They were to be lost inside the 7 million people of the Cameroun Republic or inside the 50 million people of the Republic of Nigeria. That was to make a mockery of the word "independence". Mr. Ian Grist (Cardiff, North) 20 July 1978. (House of Commons Hansard, 20 July 1978, Volume 954)

The other controversy surrounding the UN plebiscite relate to the status of the British Sothern Cameroons at the time of the plebiscite as a self-governing territory. Although the UN Charter established no criteria for determining which of the political objectives (self-government or independence) would be appropriate or adequate for a Trust Territory, Southern Cameroons had already achieved self-governing status 7 years earlier in 1954 with the Lyttleton Constitution when a House of Assembly of 13 members as well as an Executive Council were established in Buea for the Trust Territory. Thus by 1961 the UN was conducting a plebiscite in a self-governing territory with a government headed by a prime minister and a bicameral legislature. The House of Assembly at the time had been enlarged to 26 members. Given this status, it has frequently been asked; was it necessary any longer to conduct a plebiscite on independence or simply to terminate the Trusteeship Agreement and admit the Southern Cameroons into membership of the United Nations?

As concerns the ruling out of the 3rd choice in the plebiscite despite the explicit calls by the KUP and the CCC political parties for this to be included in the plebiscite, the Administering Authority gave the people of the Southern Cameroons to understand that it was the United Nations that had ruled out any 3rd option in the plebiscite, but in an interview with Dr. Foncha (former Prime Minister of Southern Cameroons) he was categorical when he told the present writer that it was in fact the British that had worked to rule out a 3rd choice (that of independence) in the UN plebiscite.

On 30th December 1998, Dr. Foncha wrote a letter to the British Secretary of State for the Foreign and Commonwealth in which he drew the attention of Her Majesty's government to the fact that in the UN Plebiscite, in British Southern Cameroons, it was the British themselves that had frustrated the aspirations of the people of Southern Cameroons to gain independence by ruling out the 3rd choice (of independence) in the plebiscite. He quoted elaborately from the declassified files on British Southern Cameroons to make his point and added:

> All political parties in the Southern Cameroons finally came to prefer independence without "joining" anybody, but the Administering Authority gave us to understand that according to the UN, it had to be by joining either Nigeria or La Republique. We were made to understand that the plebiscite was a must. In the circumstance, we wanted a 3rd choice to be included in the options. Again, the Administering Authority told us that the 3rd question was completely ruled out. The declassified files now reveal how, behind the scene, Britain worked relentlessly to thwart the 3rd option – which should have swept the votes of [an] overwhelming majority.

On the Horns of a Dilemma, the UK Discards the Expendable

On 13 August 1852 Benjamin Disraeli, Earl of Beaconsfield and later British Prime Minister wrote a letter to Lord Malmesbury in which he remarked, "these wretched colonies will all be independent too in a few years, and all a millstone round our necks." The words "wretched colonies," shows that independence had all along been regarded as an unnecessary financial burden to the colonial power like Britain. One century later in November 1960 when Mr. Lain Macleod, Secretary of State for the colonies told Foncha's government that in adopting the two alternatives of joining Nigeria or the Republic of Cameroon, the UN had ruled out separate independence for Southern Cameroons and when in response to Foncha's request that Trusteeship Agreement be extended to allow Southern Cameroons time to work towards complete independence, the Secretary of State warned the Southern Cameroons delegation against dreaming of getting the golden key of the Bank of England, he was reflecting the line of thinking of Prime Minister Benjamin Disraeli a century earlier.

One worry for the British about Southern Cameroons getting independence was that Northern Cameroons too would also have asked to be independent, and if that happened that would harm British relations with Nigeria. Such a development was something to be avoided at all cost and for that purpose "Southern Cameroons and its inhabitants" were "expendable."

The "NO" vote from Republic of Cameroon on Resolution 1608 XV came as a bolt from the blue and abruptly placed the entire United Nations decolonization process in Southern Cameroons in a dilemma. The Resolution 1608 XV being adopted to seal the fate of British Southern Cameroons proposed (paragraph 4(b)) that Southern Cameroons was to join Republic of Cameroon and the latter's vote indicated that she had rejected the proposal and such a measure could not be forced through without the consent of the Republic of Cameroon (Article 2 (7)).

Also, the post-plebiscite Conference was still pending and to attend or not to attend the conference either way was embarrassing for the UN given that Republic of Cameroon had voted against the proposed union with Southern Cameroons. The UN decided to back out of whatever remained of the plebiscite process for Southern Cameroons to join Republic of Cameroon, otherwise the UN would be participating in a conference on ceding a Trust Territory to a UN member state.

Absence of the UN

On the other hand, the Southern Cameroons electorate had been told before the plebiscite that the UN would be associated with that conference and those who were in support of joining the Republic of Cameroon had been encouraged in their choice by the idea that the United Nations was going to be present. Although the British had carefully crafted into this promise the warning that the attendance by the UN would be subject to the Organization's agreement. Many did not see this as the warning which it was intended to be. To them the UN could not possibly be heard to say "NO" on a matter concerning the decolonization of its Trust Territory and now that Republic of Cameroon had said "NO" to the UN proposal (for Southern Cameroons to join them) attendance by the UN at that Post plebiscite conference was out of the question. The Trusteeship Council Report from which Resolution 1608 XV had originated had in their report proposed the sending of three constitutional and administration experts by the General Assembly to assist the Tripartite post-plebiscite conference; paragraphs 5 and 6 of Appendix 3. But again, these experts could not go following the position taken by Republic of Cameroon on Resolution 1608 XV.

The embarrassment did not involve only the UN. The UK knew quite well that the independence of the British Cameroons had originally been arranged in accordance with the Trusteeship Agreement which she (as the Administering Authority) had set aside to propose the plebiscite which had now run into difficulty. What was needed following the Republic of Cameroon's unexpected negative vote was a tactical move to ensure that British plans of getting the entire territory of British Cameroons to join Nigeria or at least Northern Cameroons to do so, finished as planned. To finish as planned, the position of Republic of Cameroon on Resolution 1608 XV had simply to be ignored on the grounds that the majority had in effect voted for Southern Cameroons to join them. But the British had a real problem at this point in that as Administering Authority, the UK had been named in paragraph 5 of Resolution 1608 XV as part of the tripartite for drawing up the Union Constitution and Union treaty. Britain solved the problem by playing the role of a remote control, encouraging and prompting Foncha that the future of Southern Cameroons was a matter better arranged between him (Foncha) and Ahidjo as African brothers.

Clandestine Dealings between Britain and Ahidjo: Transfer of Southern Cameroons

As a Moslem from Northern Cameroon, Ahidjo's interest in the plebiscite had been to see the British Northern Cameroons (predominantly Moslems) vote to join Cameroon and when this did not happen his own dilemma too had raised up its own ugly head. It was Southern Cameroons (mainly Christians) that was coming to swell the population in the Christian South. Ahidjo also appears to have been aware not only of British refusal to Foncha's request for extension of Trusteeship but also British complaints that British Cameroons was poor and Sir Philipson's report that Southern Cameroons was economically not viable. The question by Ahidjo and his Ministers was if Southern Cameroons is a poor territory where the British would not spend their tax-payers money, why should a territory that is considered a financial burden be transferred to Republic of Cameroon? These are the circumstances behind the negative vote by Republic of Cameroon concerning the proposal for union with Southern Cameroons but this picture does not explain the ambivalence by which after voting to reject a union with Southern Cameroons, Ahidjo was suddenly sparkling with joy at the news of the ceding of the Southern Cameroons to his government.

In the midst of what was now a confusing whirlwind in Southern Cameroons' decolonization, news filtered out that oil had been discovered in large quantities on the continental shelf of the Southern Cameroons. Overnight, Southern Cameroons that had been considered to be a worthless shell of an oyster turned out to be a highly prized pearl, and Ahidjo was suddenly elated to accommodate Southern Cameroons not as a UN Trust Territory coming to join his country but as a long separated portion of his country as far back as German occupation being returned to the mother country (the Republic of Cameroon) by the United Kingdom and the United Nations. Yielding to this shallow pretext by Ahidjo, Britain ceded Southern Cameroons to French-speaking Republic of Cameroon and by that clandestine act, Britain succeeded in clearing any unnecessary burden to bear from Southern Cameroons becoming independent and expecting British financial assistance.

On the morning of 27th September 1961 therefore, the UK Ambassador accredited to Yaoundé sent a brief transfer note to the President of the Republic of Cameroon informing him that British Trusteeship in Southern Cameroons would end on the 31st of September and Southern Cameroons would be joining his country. The reply to the note came in swiftly on that same day taking note of what Ambassador C.E King had written. At the time when these brief notes were crossing the city of Yaoundé to and from the Presidency, the Secretary of State for the Colonies was informing Parliament at Westminster that at that moment that he was speaking, Southern Cameroons was being transferred to the Republic of Cameroon (not that power was being transferred to the government of the Southern Cameroons).

It should be noted here that the Exchange of Notes between the UK and the Cameroon Republic is on the "transfer" of the UN Trust Territory of the British Southern Cameroons to the Republic of Cameroon. These transfer notes expose the regrettable fact that whereas UN Resolution 1514 of 14th December 1960 on the granting of independence to colonial countries and peoples states that "immediate steps be taken (paragraph 5) in Trust and Non-Self-Governing territories to transfer all powers to the peoples of these territories without any conditions or reservations," in the process of granting independence to the British Southern Cameroons, it was the territory that was transferred to a neighbouring country, instead of transferring powers to the government of Southern Cameroons. It is obvious that this was done in order to break the political impasse created by Republic of Cameroon's negative vote on Resolution 1608 XV but it buttresses the view in this essay that British Southern

Cameroons was ceded to Republic of Cameroon. This transfer of territory (rather than power) to the people of the territory throws light on the allegation attributed to the late President Charles de Gaulle (1890 -1970) of France that the independence of British Southern Cameroons was "un petit cadeau de La Rein" and the alleged reciprocation by the Republic of Cameroon of the largest mammal (an elephant) as a pet to the Queen. The elephant ended up in a zoo in England.

No one in Southern Cameroons was informed of that business-like transaction conducted in Yaoundé about the "transfer" of Southern Cameroons to the Republic of Cameroon, not even Foncha's government. It was a deal "between sovereign governments." The Prime Minister of Southern Cameroons and Head of government, Dr. John Ngu Foncha was to know of this event (and read for himself a copy of the transfer note) 37 years later – long after he had retired from public life.

After reading the transfer note of Ambassador C.E. King for the first time, Dr. Foncha's spontaneous reaction was to question whether the purpose of the British Trusteeship was to end in the independence of British Cameroons or in the transfer of the Southern Cameroons to another country. He told the present writer how that event was not the only one in which the government and people of Southern Cameroons were kept in the dark about what was going on even though they were the subject of the transaction. He said shortly after he took office in Yaoundé as Vice-President, a British delegation came there to give Southern Cameroons' farmers destabilization funds (accumulated over the years and kept in Lagos) to the Cameroon Government. The delegation went straight and handed the money to President Ahidjo. He met the delegation afterwards and asked why they came with money that belonged to Southern Cameroons farmers and took the money to Ahidjo without bringing him (as former Prime Minister of Southern Cameroons) into the show and that he was given a cold snub with the wave of the hand: "A sovereign government deals with a sovereign government," they told him. "That money was Southern Cameroon farmers' money," said Foncha. "It was used by Ahidjo to tar streets and construct pavements in Garoua, his hometown."

It will be noted that the so-called "transfer" of the Southern Cameroons to the Republic of Cameroon was carried out in a foreign land at a time when Southern Cameroons was still a UN Trust, and without the knowledge of the government and people of the Southern Cameroons. The exchange of notes was silent about the UN plebiscite and its stated purpose of independence for Southern Cameroons. The notes said nothing concerning the status of Southern Cameroons within the Republic of Cameroon in contrast to the defined status of Northern Cameroons which had earlier joined Nigeria as a full Region (now State). Worse, the transfer note from Ambassador King brushed aside the published agreement from the bilateral talks between Foncha's government and Ahidjo's government that the instrument of sovereign powers for Southern Cameroons would be handed to an organization representing the future Cameroon Federation, not to the other partner in the Federation as was done and Southern Cameroons was automatically subordinated to the other partner in the coming federation utterly regardless of the agreement between the two states. When the British Embassy in Yaoundé received President Ahidjo's short note in the afternoon of September 27th, 1961, the UK had discarded the "expendable" (to quote from the British declassified files).

The UK and Ex-Service Men of the British Crown

During World War II, the term battlefield was expanded to include all the enemy territories, meaning that the conflict was not restricted to the territorial boundary of the nations in direct conflict in Europe but included their colonies. It also meant that human and material resources could be (and indeed were) drawn from the colonies. In Bamenda Division of the British Cameroons for example, the people raised over £181 sterling as contribution to the British War Fund, and hundreds of volunteers came forward to take up military service in the British Royal West African Frontier Force (RWAFF).

After the war, these men came back with stories of having gone so far that they saw "where the world ends." They told stirring stories from Burma and Palestine. They sang exciting songs because they were victorious and one popular song on their lips was the one about Hitler:

I have something to say
About the world war:
The war was raging
To come and conquer me:
Hitler was a bully.
He nearly knocked me down.
Every British soldier
Was fighting for The Crown.

Go and tell,
The girl whom I love
To tell my mother that she'll see me no more.
Hitler was a bully,

He nearly knocked me down.
Every British soldier
Was fighting for The Crown.

And the "British soldier" that they were singing about was not some-one from Birmingham, Manchester, or London (natives of the British Isles). Throughout the war they knew themselves not as West Africans but as British soldiers fighting for the Crown. Those of them who died, died serving The Crown.

After the war those of them from British Cameroons started an asso-ciation called the Association of Ex-Service men of the British Crown. When the present writer worked in Wum, Menchum Division where the Association of Ex-Service men of the British Crown had a branch, on the annual so-called 20th May celebration, these ex-soldiers thrilled the crowd when they marched. Their style of marching was (characteristic of age) a little awkward but the military commands from their leader and the proud swing of his arms as he came forward alone to salute the Senior Divisional Officer were reminiscent of that spritely display seen on the annual Queen's birth day parade in London. All seated in the grand stand would rise as he approached the VIPs and there would be a big spontaneous outburst of applause to cheer and honour him and his men. He would raise his hand in military salute and looking at the Senior Divisional Officer announce in English "Ex-Service men of the British Crown, sah." A deafening applause would greet him and his men again as he proudly marched back to resume command.

These were the men who proudly served the British Crown and came back proud of their service and victory in the war. They were the men who had jumped in and out of trenches during the war. They were the men whose faces had been marred by mud, sweat and blood, fighting for The British Crown. Their fellow countrymen who fell in battle had fought for The Crown and made the supreme sacrifice. If ever you told any of these men that the very Crown for whom they fought in the war will turn around after the war was won and betray them in what was "THE SUPREME WAR" to set their own country free, he would have called you the world's tallest liar.

A few years after the war ended these soldiers came home and the name of one of them (Francis Dohmatob, a cousin of the present writer) was headline on the front pages of newspapers throughout Nigeria and the British Southern Cameroons. He had received a letter from Her Majesty the Queen. The letter was sent through the Governor General of Nigeria in Lagos who doubled as High Commissioner for the British

Southern Cameroons which was something rare for an ordinary soldier of no rank. The whole (extended) family including the present writer gathered to hear the content of the letter from the Her Majesty. It was a short letter of congratulations from the Sovereign on the birth of a triplet by Na Manyi, Dohmatob's wife. Na Manyi had not made any ominous suggestion to her mother-in-law like the one in the Hitler song. She only waited patiently for his return, and 10 months after his arrival home they were both to be seen over the happy faces of their triplets humming a lullaby to the babies. Francis Domatob was fond of the Hitler song and frequently sang it long after the arrival of the triplets. If you had told him that The Crown for whom they fought with loyalty in the war would turn round fifteen years later and jettison them together with their country in what was "The Supreme War" to grant freedom to their own country, he would have called you the double-horned devil from hell.

In December 1960, the UN declared in resolution 1514 (XV) that the subjection of peoples to subjugation, domination and exploitation constitutes a denial of fundamental human rights and that "immediate steps shall be taken in Trust and Non-Self- Governing Territories to transfer all powers to the peoples of those territories without any conditions or reservation." The British Southern Cameroon was a Self-Governing UN Trust Territory at the time of this declaration. The Federal Republic of Cameroon which Ahidjo signed and promulgated into law in Southern Cameroons was formed by the State of former Southern Cameroons which became West Cameroon and former Republic of Cameroon which became East Cameroon. When the East Cameroon seceded from that Federation in 1984 and took up her former name and identity as Republic of Cameroon, that Federation was defunct. Southern Cameroons could not federate alone, and they did the only thing which any other group of people would do in that circumstance: they responded by also resuming their own former identity as Southern Cameroons. This was like the story of the pig and the baboon:

> Long ago the pig and the baboon lived together on the hillsides. One day it was very cold, and a cutting wind was blowing. As the pig and the baboon sat in the sun trying to get warm, the baboon turned to the pig, and said, "This wind is enough to wear the end of one's nose to a blunt point."
>
> "Yes," answered the pig, "it's really enough to blow the hairs off one's buttocks and leave a bare, dry patch."

"Look here," said the baboon, getting crossed, "you are not to make personal remarks!"

"I did nothing of the kind," retorted the pig, but you were rude to me first."

This started a quarrel, and the two concluded that neither cared for the other's company. So, they parted, and the baboon went up on the rocky top of the hill, while the pig went down to the plains, and there, they remained to this day.

The Republic of Cameroon and Southern Cameroons can learn from what the pig and the baboon did finally. Instead of warning the other not to secede or pointing to the other that you already seceded in 1984 why don't we sit down and dialogue as the international community, the Commonwealth and the Francophonie have all proposed? Why use the gun to solve a political question? *And what justification has the Republic of Cameroon on its territorial claim on Southern Cameroons?*

If we can admit that for half a century now, we have stirred this our bowl of palm oil and water and it just cannot (and will not) blend, why can't we accept the fact that no matter how long we go on stirring, this water and palm oil will never ever blend? After the carnage of 2017, any hope of Southern Cameroons and Republic of Cameroon ever succeeding in unifying is inconceivable. In the 2017 escalation (and typical of all dictators) Mr. Biya hastened to state that the form of the Cameroon State was not negotiable. In saying this, he forgot that by Article 47 of the 1961 Constitution of the Federal Republic of Cameroon, that Federation was entrenched and any proposal for the revision of that Constitution which impaired the unity and integrity of the Federation was declared "inadmissible." What happened to that Federation?

Independence by Joining: Cold Shoulder and Veto

"Members of the United Nations which have or assume responsibilities for the administration of territories whose peoples have not yet attained a full measure of self-government recognize the principle that the interests of the inhabitants of these territories are paramount, and accept as a sacred trust the obligation to promote to the utmost within the system of international peace and security established by the present Charter, the well-being of the inhabitants of these territories, and, to this end:

a. To ensure with due respect the culture of the peoples concerned, their political economic, social and educational advancement, their just treatment, and their protection against abuses.

b. To develop self-government, to take due account of the political aspirations of the peoples and to assist them in the progressive development of their free political institutions..." (Article 73 of the UN Charter).

Southern Cameroons was obviously used in the process of decolonization to foster colonial interest either in safeguarding future friendship with Nigeria or in the desire to tidy Nigeria's frontiers from Lake Chad to the sea and of course, friendship with the Republic of Cameroon by ceding the Southern Cameroons to the government of that country, all of which led to the obliteration of British Cameroons. In all these we see nothing of interest for the inhabitants of the territory. We see nothing of the acceptance of a sacred trust on the part of the Administering Authority to assist the people of British Southern Cameroons towards their aspiration. All Trust Territories had a common aspiration: Independence. What is irrefutably clear in the case of British Cameroons is that their aspiration to achieve independence was frustrated by using a plebiscite about independence as window dressing but firmly ruling out the option of independence. More than that, it is crystal clear that whereas the purpose and goal of decolonization was to assist countries under colonial rule become independent (achieve self-determination) the decolonization of British Southern Cameroons transported that territory and its inhabitants from colonial rule into servitude and completely obliterated that UN Trust Territory from existence. The irony is that this process was carried out from start to finish under the supervision of the United Nations itself.

This new road map on decolonization via a plebiscite not only transported British Cameroons to a dead end but placed both the UN and the UK visibly on the horns of a dilemma: The UN could not (on the recommendation of the Administering Authority) spend time and resources to conduct a plebiscite on independence and at the end of the exercise turn round to grant that independence of the British Southern Cameroons according to the Charter and the Trusteeship Agreement because the Republic of Cameroon had voted against Southern Cameroons joining her. Equally a dead end was the alternative of getting the Republic of Cameroon to accept the Southern Cameroons after she had voted "No" on that proposal in Resolution 1608 XV. In the circumstance the UN backed out and the UK ceded the territory to the Republic of Cameroon. That is the fact that is as clear as day light. The words of the British Minister of State on 12th October 1961 in his minutes to Sir John Martin that "The Southern Cameroons and its inhabitants are expendable," were obviously not compatible with British undertaking in Article 73 of the charter.

One person who clearly saw what was going wrong with the decolonization of British Cameroons was Mr. Dag Hammarskjold the Secretary General of the United Nations from 1953-61. He died in a plane crash in the Congo shortly after he visited Buea to discuss the Southern Cameroons plebiscite. Mr. Hammarskjold had come to realize that the plan to conduct a plebiscite in British Cameroons did not only violate Article 73 of the UN charter quoted above but was entirely wrong. It was wrong because the plebiscite changed what was declared in the charter about the International Trusteeship system. Indeed, the plebiscite on independence by joining was going to be a negation of the basic principle of the International Trusteeship System.

FIGURE 2.1. Dag Hammarskjold, 1905 – 1961, Secretary General of the United Nations, 1953 – 1961

It was also a dangerous thing for the UN to dangle a small territory wedged between two bigger countries like a bait with the tempting prospect of territorial expansion for the two bigger nations. Some reflection on Mr. Hammarskjold's part had led to the conclusion that the UN plebiscite was shaping a potential conflict in future between Nigeria and Cameroon and it became clear to him that the plebiscite in British Cameroons was a big mistake. He therefore proposed to call a round-table meeting of all the stake-holders to find a way out. Since the decision on the plebiscite had been taken, it could still be conducted, and its purpose and focus modified to enable British Cameroons to achieve her independence. The British administrators in Buea "threw cold water" on the idea insisting that the plebiscite had to go ahead as planned[1].

We saw earlier that one of the choices in the plebiscite prescribed a post-plebiscite conference to work out details of the constitutional arrangements for the union between the Republic of Cameroon and that part of British Cameroons that would vote in favour of joining the Republic of Cameroon.

Northern Cameroons voted in favour of joining Nigeria and Southern Cameroons in favour of joining the Republic of Cameroon and time came for the post-plebiscite conference. Both the UK and the UN did not show up for the conference and there has never been a statement as to why the UK and the UN did not attend as promised. It is likely that the idea that the UN plebiscite in British Cameroons was a mistake lingered on in New York after the death of Dag Hammarskjold. The mistake itself got compounded by the vote by the Republic of Cameroon rejecting union with the Southern Cameroons.

In anticipation of their absence from the post-plebiscite conference the British had prepared a safety valve. According to The Two Alternatives (op. cit.) the conditions for the UN to attend the conference was that the organization would first agree to do so:

> .... It being understood that the association of the United Nations with the post-plebiscite conference mentioned in

---

1 "Mr Hammarskjold was afraid lest a difficult security situation should arise and was anxious to avoid anything in the nature of a 'contest between two independent states' (Nigeria and the Republic). He was wondering therefore whether it would not be a good thing for him to summon about March a "round table discussion" between Ahidjo, Foncha, Endeley and representatives of Nigeria. It might then be possible to work out some formula which would avoid the necessity for any plebiscite. The formula could however be tested by a plebiscite if the United Nations so wanted. We criticized this idea rather sharply"(*British declassified files*).

the text below would be subject to its agreement.

A vote for attaining independence by joining the Republic would mean that by an early date to be decided by the United Nations after consultation with the government of the Southern Cameroons, the Cameroons Republic and the United Kingdom as administering Authority, The Southern Cameroons and the Cameroun Republic would unite in a Federal United Cameroon Republic. The arrangement would be worked out after the plebiscite by a conference consisting of representative delegation of equal status from the Republic and the Southern Cameroons. The United Nations and the United Kingdom would also be associated with this Conference.

Thus, according to this British arrangement, if the UN did not attend the conference there was already an explanation: the UN had not agreed after all. What must be said to debunk this is simple: nobody in Southern Cameroons (or elsewhere) ever heard afterwards that the UN refused to attend the post-plebiscite conference either.

On the contrary at the United Nations, the Report of the Trusteeship Council of 18 April 4.2 (4) affirmed the tutelary authority of the UN over the Southern Cameroons when it recommended in paragraphs five and six of its report as follows:

> 5. Invites the Administering Authority, the Government of the Southern Cameroons and the Republic of Cameroon to initiate urgent discussions with a view to finalizing before 1 October 1961, the arrangement by which the agreed and declared policies of the concerned parties for a union of the Southern Cameroons with the Republic of Cameroon into a Federal United Cameroon Republic will be implemented.

> 6. Appoints a Commission of three constitutional and administrative experts to be nominated one each by three Member States designated by the General Assembly to assist in the discussion referred to in paragraph 5 above." (Appendix 3).

Three days later on 21 April 1961, this report from the Trusteeship Council was adopted by the General Assembly of the UN as Resolution 1608 XV without paragraph six quoted above. This was unusual. In the functioning of the United Nations Resolutions from the Trusteeship Council were usually adopted by the General Assembly without further amendments because right from the start, the Trusteeship Council consisted of: Representatives of all UN members administering Trust Territories, the five permanent members of the Security Council (China, France, the Soviet Union/Russia Federation, UK and the USA). As many other non-administering members as needed to equalize the number of administering and non-administering members, elected by the UN General Assembly for a 3-year renewable term. This means that the Trusteeship Council was the one organ in the United Nations in which all five veto-members of the Security Council participated and if therefore the Council reached a decision on a point, this was certain to be adopted in the General Assembly without further amendments. But the crucial paragraph 6 of the Trusteeship Council report quoted above reminding the United Nations to honour its commitments to the people of the BSC was surprisingly dropped and paragraph 5 that was adopted has regrettably never been implemented. The entire Resolution 1608 XV has remained unimplemented since it was adopted."

UN (GA) Resolution 1608 XV

We come now to consider why Resolution 1608 XV was adopted in the General Assembly without paragraph 6 (the last paragraph) of the Trusteeship Council Report. Before we do this, let's look closely at the content of the entire Resolution 1608 XV (Appendix 4).

The Resolution addresses four issues:

First, it endorses the result of the plebiscite in both Northern and Southern Cameroons. Northern Cameroons, the Resolution states, had voted by a substantial majority to achieve independence by joining the independent Federation of Nigeria and Southern Cameroons had similarly decided to achieve independence by joining the independent Republic of Cameroon. It is important to note here that in both paragraphs 2(a) and 2(b) of the Resolution, the Resolution states that the people had voted "to achieve independence" which, in so far as the people of Southern Cameroons were concerned, was the key reason for their voting in the Plebiscite. The resolution then goes on to set different dates for terminating the Trusteeship Agreement of 13 December 1961 on British Cameroons: 1 June 1961 for Northern Cameroon and 1 October 1961 for Southern Cameroons. Concerning Southern Cameroons specifically, the Resolution goes on in paragraph five to invite the Administering Authority, the Government of the Southern Cameroons and Republic of Cameroon to initiate urgent discussions with a view to finalizing before 1 October 1961 the arrangements by which the agreed and declared polices of the parties concerned would be implemented.

So, what happened to paragraph six of the Trusteeship Council report quoted above? One possible explanation is that the negative vote by the Republic of Cameroon on UN proposal for BSC to join the Republic of Cameroon meant that she had not given her consent for BSC to join her and in the circumstance could no longer participate in a conference which was in effect surrendering or ceding a UN Trust Territory to a UN member-state that had explicitly registered her objection to a union with British Southern Cameroons.

Because the plebiscite questions were a call on the people to express themselves on achieving independence, there was massive participation. The present writer had the privilege of participating and served as polling officer. We were selected in January 1961 and attended public meetings where the process of voting was very thoroughly explained and rehearsed especially on checking and ticking of voters' names in the electoral register. There were two ballot boxes one white and the other green for choice of Republic of Cameroon and Nigeria respectively. Each voter's name was checked on the electoral register, his/her name ticked off on the list and hand marked with indelible ink and he/she was then given a ballot paper to go in and vote.

The result of the plebiscite in the Southern Cameroons was in favour of Southern Cameroons joining the Republic of Cameroon and in Northern Cameroons for that territory joining Nigeria. The results were as follows:

TABLE 2.1. The score board county by county of the 1961 UN plebiscite in Southern Cameroons

	For Nigeria	For Cameroon
Southern Cameroons	97,741	233,571
Northern Cameroons	146,296	97,659

It is also clear that while each of the 97 countries that participated in voting on Resolution 1608 XV was voting FOR or AGAINST Southern Cameroons achieving independence by joining Republic of Cameroon, the vote of Republic of Cameroon on this Resolution had an additional significance namely, giving her consent for the Southern Cameroons to join her or denying her consent. This additional significance is rooted in Article 2 (7) of the Charter. This Article states the UN's principle of non-interference in the internal issues of member states: "*Nothing contained in the present Charter shall authorize the United Nations to intervene in matters which are essentially within the domestic jurisdiction of any state or the Members to submit such matters to settlement under the present Charter...*"(2, 7). In effect, here was a proposed union being imposed by the UN on a member state (Republic of Cameroon) by which that State was to be required to change its existing unitary system of government to a federal one with the federal union of two states both being equal in status. Republic of Cameroon was going to surrender its sovereign status to the impending federation and become extinct from the international scene and from the UN as well. Republic of Cameroon could give (or deny) her consent on the proposal and significantly she voted "NO" to the Resolution and its proposals in paragraph 4(b) that Southern Cameroons should join her.

France and all her former African colonies did not support Southern Cameroons independence on this resolution and nearly all French speaking states in Africa including the Republic of Cameroon (partner in the impending Federal United Cameroon Republic) voted "No" to Southern Cameroon's independence and "No" to her joining the Republic of Cameroon. However, when the discovery of oil in British Southern Cameroon was made public around this time, France made a U-turn on Southern Cameroons joining its former colony. France now advised Ahidjo's government to work towards the annexation and assimilation of the Anglophones which practically meant territorial expansion to the west and a grip on Southern Cameroons' newly discovered oil wells. France saw nothing but national gains in protecting President Ahidjo remaining in power in Cameroon. Above all, France was to initiate a policy that no Anglophone (Southern Cameroonian) should ever aspire to the presidency in Cameroon which should remain the reserve of Francophones. In 1992, when John Fru Ndi won the presidential elections in Cameroon, he was placed under house arrest for 3 months while Paul Biya who was defeated in that election was sworn in. France drew the red line policy which Anglophones in Cameroon were never to cross. Should the people of Cameroon ever make the mistake in future to vote for John Fru Ndi or an Anglophone to the presidency, France would step in with arms to restore the status quo.

Resolution 1608 XV was adopted by the General Assembly by a vote of 64 for and 23 against with 10 abstentions. And after adopting the Resolution it has remained unimplemented while Republic of Cameroon tells the world that in 1961 the UK and the UN returned a part of their country to them. Some people have criticized the working of the UN on the grounds that since this resolution carried a UN proposal (paragraph 4b) for Southern Cameroons to join Republic of Cameroon and the latter had voted against the resolution it meant that the Republic of Cameroon did not give her consent on the proposed union with the Southern Cameroons that was not present herself at this transaction. Therefore, the state of the Southern Cameroons should not have been forced to join the Republic of Cameroon. The proposed Union should have automatically been aborted and Southern Cameroons granted her independence in accordance with the Trusteeship Agreement and Article 76 of the Charter.

It can of course be argued that once the majority (64) voted to adopt the resolution, the vote of the Republic of Cameroon against was of no consequence. Surely not in this particular case (the critics argue) because having openly registered her opposition to Southern Cameroons joining her, it meant that the presence of the UN and/or the UK as Administering Authority participating in any conference after this vote would only be interpreted as ceding a UN Trust Territory to a member State who had openly rejected the union. It is in this light that the single "NO" vote by Republic of Cameroon on an issue that directly affected her sovereignty was equivalent to the veto of a permanent member in the Security Council. The critics conclude that when Southern Cameroons was compelled to join Republic of Cameroon in spite of the latter's opposition it was like a rash traffic violation in which the UN wagon carrying British Southern Cameroons came crashing at the frontier check points of the Republic of Cameroon in total disregard of speed breaks and red warning lights flashing visibly ahead. The disaster following in the wake of the UN imposed union in Cameroon then should come as no surprise because we know what happens when the driver of a speeding truck ignores all safety measures on a road where caution is advised. Yet the UK is not the driver that should be told anything about "the interest of the inhabitants" (Article 73 of the Charter) of a colonial territory. At the end of British rule in the Crown Colony of Hong Kong, the UK could hold up Hong Kong to the world with pride as an example of how to take good care of the future (and interest) of a people. In the decolonization of the British Southern Cameroons however, the United Kingdom exerted all effort to prevent Southern Cameroons becoming independent.

The emergence of Boko-Haram insurgency in what was British Northern Cameroon and the Catapult Revolution in what was British Southern Cameroons both tell the story of a failed decolonization. How? If British Cameroon got its own independence as the rest of British

CEDED AT DAWN

colonies in West Africa did, the world should have been spared of the
two conflicts in the sub-region.

As stated above Mr. Dag Hammarskjold clearly saw that things had
gone the wrong way for British Cameroons. He threw the weight of his
position as Secretary General of the UN to correct what was going wrong
and the disaster that inevitably was to follow, but he was cut short by
death and British Southern Cameroons emerged from the process of
decolonization not independent or self-governing, but recolonized by
an independent African country whose colonial history was similar to
British Southern Cameroons. Worse than that, Republic of Cameroon
the new colonial master with the backing of France and the UK was to
lay a dramatic claim to the territory of the Southern Cameroons and
carry out an invasion and genocide to assert its territorial claim.

Mr. Hammarskjöld was not the only one who saw that the UN plebiscite in Southern Cameroons was a big mistake. In the British House of
Commons debate on August 1, 1961, The Honourable G.M. Thomson,
(MP for Dundee East and later Member of the House of Lords) drew
the attention of the British Parliament to this:

> As I was saying, I was anxious to raise with the Government
> the situation in the Southern Cameroons. As the House will
> know, this is a Territory for which we operate a trusteeship
> under the United Nations. The Southern Cameroons chose
> in a United Nations plebiscite on 11th February of this year
> to join with the Cameroun Republic, a former French Ter-
> ritory. The United Nations in its wisdom decided that the
> union between the Southern Cameroons and the Cameroun
> Republic should take place on 1st October this year. This is
> a very short period indeed even in the most favourable cir-
> cumstances but the circumstances here, as the Minister will
> agree, are in many ways anything but favourable.
>
> The problem of uniting these two territories would in any
> event be difficult. They are two territories of completely
> different cultures, with different political systems, the one
> English-speaking and the other French-speaking in the lan-
> guage of its administration. There are extremely complex
> problems in bringing these two countries together within
> one national State. So far as I can discover, no serious work
> has been done on joining these countries and getting down
> to the hard problems of bringing them together. So far only

a number of very general declarations have been made about the kind of framework that might be proposed. In these circumstances a potentially very dangerous situation has arisen."

Honourable Thomson went on to say:

Before I come to the suggestions I wish to put before the Government for dealing with the matter, it is only fair to try to measure up what the Government's responsibilities have been and how far they have fulfilled them. It is a pretty poor story. The Government had ample warning of the difficulties which were mounting up in the Southern Cameroons. Month after month has gone and indeed year after year. We are now within a few weeks of 1st October and nothing effective has been done to ensure that this Territory, into which we have put much work, will have a reasonable chance of going forward into a prosperous and peaceful future.

The Government have been guilty of neglect in a number of different instances. They should have fought much harder than they did at the United Nations in the Trusteeship Council for a third choice being offered to the peoples of the Southern Cameroons when the plebiscite took place. The fact was that both the Prime Minister of the Southern Cameroons and the Leader of the Opposition there, though they had same differences between themselves, were anxious that there should be sufficient breathing space for the Southern Cameroons to negotiate with the Cameroun Republic proper arrangements for union and that they should not be suddenly forced into the kind of union which may well be thrust upon them without adequate preparation.

I appreciate the difficulties of our getting our way in the Trusteeship Council of the United Nations, but it does not seem to me from reading the debates there and from what I have been able to gather that Her Majesty's Government made nearly a big enough effort to back up the elected leaders of the Southern Cameroons in facing up to this problem." (House of Commons Hansard, August 1 1961, Column 1341)

In the debate, Lord Thomson showed the consequences of leaving the

Southern Cameroons with an uncertain future and how it was not late to avert the impending catastrophe. Unfortunately, the British Government had failed to carry out its responsibility in the Trusteeship Agreement, he asked the British Government to tell Parliament whether the people of the Southern Cameroons could not have been given a wider choice in the plebiscite.

The reply from the government side was by the Under Secretary of State for the Colonies Mr. Hughes Fraser who told Parliament that the United Nations had decided that the choice in the Plebiscite was either to join Nigeria or to join the independent Republic. Mr. Frazer's reply was of course a lie (a white one), and nothing shows dirt like a white lie. Dr. Foncha's letter of 30th December 1998 to the Secretary of State for Foreign and Commonwealth was to quote copiously from the British declassified files to show that the British Government fought hard against a third choice in the Southern Cameroons plebiscite. And it must be added that the third question – that of outright independence without joining an adjacent State – was certain to win overwhelmingly in the plebiscite.

Before his death, Dr. Kevin Gumne and the present writer had the rare privilege of meeting with Lord Thomson in London. Our conversation at dinner offered by Lord Thomson fell naturally on the August 1st 1961 House of Commons debate and his speech during that debate. He was somewhat surprised when we mentioned the name of Mr. Hughes Frazer and asked us where we got a copy of that his speech and the details about who else spoke, and we told him from the UK House of Commons Historic Hansard. He was interested in knowing how British Cameroons and French Cameroons had adjusted together since the former joined the latter, and our conversation turned naturally to matters of assimilation, and marginalization in Cameroon:

"My Lord, imagine that one morning the people of this Country woke up to hear BBC broadcasting a decree signed by Her Majesty the Queen changing the name of this country from United Kingdom to England without consulting anyone from Scotland or the other parts of the country. How would the Scots for example take it?"

Lord Thomson leaned forward letting lose his great sense of humour. "And you are saying this to a Scot!! War! That would be war!!"

War was indeed to come (not from the frequent change of name and flag which signified instability of the country but) from an astonishing invasion engendered by a baseless territorial claim by the Republic of Cameroon over British Southern Cameroons with the complicity of France and the UK.

PART III

&

VIRTUALLY AT WAR
THROUGHOUT

Chapter 3

TRUTH: THE FIRST CASUALTY OF THE WAR

The level of human rights violations, mistrust and marginalization between the two former UN Trust Territories in Cameroon did not from the beginning express themselves in the use of guns but it was war nonetheless, and Republic of Cameroon used her status as a sovereign state with worldwide diplomatic connections to misinform and falsify what was actually happening in Cameroon. Indeed, the political association of British Southern Cameroons with the French speaking Republic of Cameroon perfectly illustrates the statement that in times of war the first casualty is ***truth***.

However, facts do not cease to be facts just because they have been falsified. What follows is an outline of some aspects of the falsification of the history of the British Southern Cameroons by the Republic of Cameroon during the period of the annexation. Facts are stubborn things. They can be suppressed for some time but not for all times. Before we take up this directly let us say something about bias words. Bias words in language are those words which show a slanted judgment or view intended to influence listeners (or readers) against or in favour of one view. Thus, in Cameroon words like secession, secessionist, separatists, Anglophone, radicals, extremist are prejudiced words intended to bias opinion against English speaking people of the North West and South West regions.

The Statehood of the Southern Cameroons UN Trust Territories

We will start with the statehood of The British Southern Cameroons and its territory as defined by international Treaties. This UN trust territory, formally the League of Nations mandated territory under British administration was granted independence by the United Nations General Assembly under UN (GA) 1608 XV to take effect from 1st October 1961 by joining the Republic of Cameroon. Before attaining this status, British Southern Cameroons had attained (and enjoyed) self-governing status as far back as 26th October 1954 as part of Nigeria. When Nigeria attained independence on 1st October 1960, British Southern Cameroons separated from Nigeria as a separate self-governing State and during the year 1960 – 1961 the Southern Cameroons was no longer a part of Nigeria and was not ruled from the Republic of Cameroon either. Southern Cameroons was a self-governing state with its complete international boundaries.

It is necessary to point out here in passing that the Southern Cameroons is not the southern part of the Republic of Cameroon, although the two states are former United Nations trust territories. The territory of Southern Cameroons is defined by international treaties and described in international instruments such as the League of Nations Mandate and the United Nations Trusteeship Agreement.

Although the Southern Cameroons was formally granted independence by the United Nations General Assembly, this independence did not take effect as envisaged principally because both the United Nations and the United Kingdom abandoned the process of the decolonization of British Southern Cameroons without completing the process of the plebiscite that was conducted for that purpose. Furthermore, Resolution 1608 XV was adopted but never implemented and from 1961 the two territories kept co-habiting informally until 1984 when President Paul Biya withdrew East Cameroon from the informal union and renamed it the Republic of Cameroon. Southern Cameroons could not federate alone.

Over the years after her secession from the defunct Union in 1984 the Republic of Cameroon has misinformed the world that the southern part of her country was trying to secede. The Republic of Cameroon claims that in 1961 the United Nations and the United Kingdom returned the southern part of her country to her. This was absolutely false as Southern Cameroons had never been part of the Republic of Cameroon.

Independence or Re-unification

As we have narrated so far, in 1961 the United Nations conducted a plebiscite in Southern Cameroons on Independence (not Re-unification). After that plebiscite the United Nations pronounced itself on Southern Cameroons independence (endorsing the decision of the people of BSC to become independent). Over the years, the Republic of Cameroon has made it a policy to harass, arrest and torture Southern Cameroonians for coming out to celebrate the anniversary of their independence on 1st October[1].

---

1   During the 2017 anniversary, the level of killings by the armed forces deployed throughout the Southern Cameroons amounted to a genocide. (See select newspaper front page coverage, page 67).

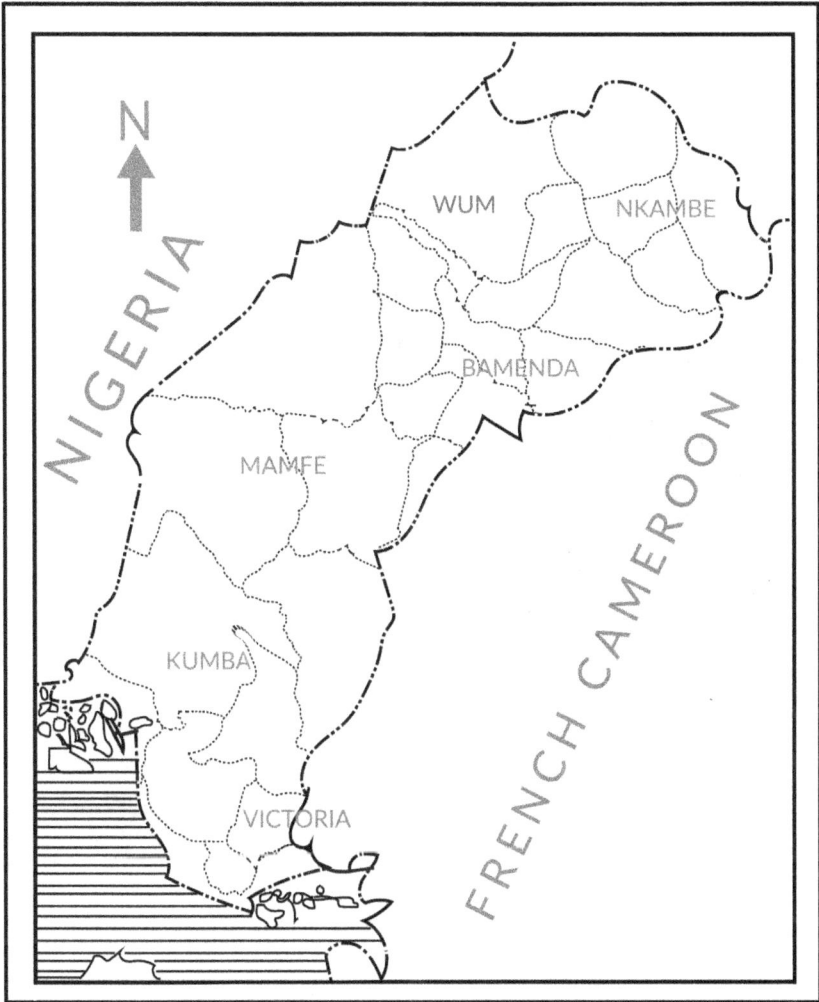

International boundaries .—..—..—..—..—..—.
Divisional boundaries   ....

FIGURE 3.1 Map of the Southern Cameroons showing the territory's international boundaries

FIGURE 3.2. The Hon Dr. E.M.L Endeley, OBE, First Prime Minister of the Southern Cameroons

FIGURE 3.3. Parliamentary session in the Southern Cameroons House of Assembly in Buea

FIGURE 3.4. Mr. John Ngu Foncha, Second Prime Minister of the Southern Cameroons inspecting a Guard of Honour in Buea, Southern Cameroons

When the United Nations conducted the 11th February 1961 Plebiscite in British Southern Cameroons the questions asked were:

"Do you wish to achieve Independence by joining the independent Federation of Nigeria"

OR

"Do you wish to achieve Independence by joining the independent Republic of Cameroon?"

The purpose of the UN Plebiscite was not (repeat, not) on the integration of BSC into Nigeria or Republic of Cameroon. It was on **independence**. It was not to reconstitute the old German Cameroon, parts of which are today in surrounding countries. It was a plebiscite about Southern Cameroons' independence, clear and simple.

The people of Southern Cameroons voted in favour of the second choice, so let us look closely at that choice and at what happened after the plebiscite. There are two important things to note in the question: *independence* and *joining* (not re-unification).

Independence

After the plebiscite, the General Assembly sat on 21st April 1961 and adopted Resolution 1608 XV. This UN Resolution shows in paragraph 2 that the UN "endorsed the results of the plebiscite that the peoples of the Southern Cameroons have decided to achieve independence."

So, did the UN grant independence to the Southern Cameroons? The answer is a "Yes" even if (as it happens) the people of Southern Cameroons do not enjoy that independence. The United Nations went further in paragraph 4(b) of that resolution 1608 XV to name 1st October as the date for termination of the Trusteeship Agreement (effective date of independence for Southern Cameroons).

Joining

The first thing to note here, is that the word "joining" (used by the UN) and the word "Re-unification" (used by the Republic of Cameroon both referring to the same event in 1961 do not mean the same thing. The latter is used by the Republic of Cameroon to falsify the event which the former (by the United Nations) describes. We will steer clear of the word "Re-unification" and discuss the word used by the United Nations. The plebiscite question was "Do you wish to achieve Independence by joining the independent Republic of Cameroon?"- in paragraph 4(b) of UN Resolution 1608 XV, the UN proposed that in conformity with their choice at the plebiscite the Southern Cameroons should join Republic of Cameroon and (to the surprise of everyone in Southern Cameroons) Republic of Cameroon voted "NO" to that Resolution and the proposal it contained which means that the Republic of Cameroon did not want Southern Cameroons to join her as proposed.

The UN (as mentioned earlier) was thrown into embarrassment by this unexpected official stance by Republic of Cameroon. Why? Because in accordance with Article 2 (7) of the UN Charter the UN cannot enforce a decision that affects the internal matter of a member state (as the federation arrangement of the plebiscite was going to do with Republic of Cameroon's centralized system) unless that member gives its consent.

The "NO" vote by the Republic of Cameroon meant that the International experiment on "Independence by joining" had completely failed in Cameroon. It was now left for the UN to either abort "Independence by joining" and grant the independence of the Southern Cameroons strictly on the road map in the Charter and the Trusteeship Agreement as had originally been envisaged or ask the Republic of Cameroon to reconsider her "NO" vote on that Resolution. The UN did neither of these. Instead, the UN asked the Administering Authority (who had recommended the conducting of the plebiscite) to handle the problem. The UK resolved the impasse by ceding the Southern Cameroons to the Republic of Cameroon on 27th September 1961 disregarding their expressed rejection of the proposal that Southern Cameroons should join her.

The implication of Nigeria's "YES" vote on Resolution 1608 XV

On Resolution 1608 XV Nigeria voted "YES" which means that Nigeria gave her consent for Northern Cameroons to join her while The Republic of Cameroon voted "No" on the same set of proposals by the United Nations. Thus, by transferring the Southern Cameroons to the Republic of Cameroon nonetheless the United Kingdom as the Administering Authority treated the different positions taken by the Republic of Cameroon and the Federal Republic of Nigeria as if "No" and "Yes" were synonyms. The People of Southern Cameroons submit that the positions taken by the Republic of Cameroon with a "NO" vote called for the process of "independence by joining" to be aborted in the case of the Southern Cameroons and the territory given her independence based on the Charter and the Trusteeship Agreement as was originally envisaged. The wrong action that was taken is the root cause of the invasion and genocide in Southern Cameroons and the long-term solution to the conflict is the restoration of the separate independence of British Southern Cameroons.

Post-plebiscite Conference or Foumban Conference

On Thursday 20th February 2014 the importance of the Foumban Conference of July 1961 was emphasized not only by President Biya in his address at Buea (in the so-called re-unification celebration) but by Cameroon Radio and Television (CRTV) journalists like Charles Ndongo, who repeatedly commented that many people in Southern Cameroons still did not know what was decided in Foumban. However, the following points must be noted by all who value authentic history and reliable information:

First, the Foumban Conference was not the UN post-plebiscite Conference prescribed by the United Nations General Assembly in paragraph 5 of UN (GA) Resolution 1608 XV. The UN General Assembly had prescribed a post-plebiscite International Conference comprising the United Kingdom as Administering Authority, the Government of the Southern Cameroons and the Government of the Republic of Cameroon. Thus, one of the key conditions for Southern Cameroons joining the Republic of Cameroon clearly stated by the United Nations was the convening of a post-plebiscite conference which was to be international

in composition. This condition is contained in the plebiscite manifesto:
The Two Alternatives

In this plebiscite manifesto, the British Colonial Secretary states this condition as follows:

> A vote for attaining independence by joining the Republic would mean that by an early date to be decided by the United Nations after consultation with the government of the Southern Cameroons, the Cameroons Republic and the United Kingdom as administering Authority, The Southern Cameroons and the Cameroon Republic would unite in a Federal United Cameroon Republic. The arrangement would be worked out after the plebiscite by a conference consisting of representative delegation of equal status from the Republic and the Southern Cameroons. The United Nations and the United Kingdom would also be associated with this Conference.

It can be seen from the above that whereas the condition of independence in Nigeria were fore-closed in the Nigerian offer of a full Regional status equal to other Regions in Nigeria as re-echoed on Sunday 22nd January, 1961 in a radio broadcast on the Southern Cameroons plebiscite by the Prime Minister of the Federation of Nigeria, Sir Abubakar Tafawa Balewa, the condition for joining the Republic of Cameroon were still subject to negotiation and apparently under very favourable conditions.

Also, the prospect of first attaining independence and sovereignty was implied in Mr. McLeod's statement that the Southern Cameroons and the Republic of Cameroon were to meet in delegations of equal status. Since the Republic of Cameroon was already sovereign, it implied ipso facto that the Southern Cameroons would be sovereign before or by the date of the conference.

After the plebiscite and without implementing the General Assembly's directives in Resolution 1608 XV the British government, as the Administering Authority, also withdraw her troops, personnel and they packed their bags and baggage and abandoned the territory leaving it defenseless without handing over the Trust properly to the beneficiary, Prime Minister John Ngu Foncha, the legally constituted authority in the Southern Cameroons.

To further aggravate an already very bad situation, the British Government on September 27th 1961 through Ambassador C.K. King serving in Yaounde, ceded the Southern Cameroons to the Republic of Cameroon not even to the Federal United Cameroon Republic as had been agreed upon by the parties in their bilateral talks. This action was in total breach of United Nations Resolution 2013 (XXVI) of 31st May 1960.

Taking advantage of the United Kingdom's blunder of abandonment and gross dereliction of duty to its former Trust Territory, the Republic of Cameroon on September 30th, 1961 shrewdly and illegally moved in troops and gendarmes and occupied the Southern Cameroons territory and annexed it. Resistance to assimilation and the introduction of French laws and education in Southern Cameroon culminated in the 2017 invasion and genocide

What took place in Foumban lacked international validity which the post-plebiscite conference by the United Nations was going to have. Both the plebiscite manifesto (*The Two Alternatives*) and paragraph 6 of the report of the Trusteeship Council on 18 April 1961 are clear that the United Nations was due to send constitutional and administrative experts to the post-plebiscite conference. This emphasizes the international character of that conference. Foumban was cross-current on UN plans. It was the setting at which UN decolonization of the Southern Cameroons was turned into annexation.

Two Views on the Annexation of the Southern Cameroons

First the independent view of Mr. Pierre Mesmer in *Les Blancs s'en Vont*. Mr. Pierre Messmer was one-time Governor of French Cameroon (1956-57), who later became France's Minister for the Armed Forces, and still later, French Prime Minister. He was the first independent observer to tell the world that British Southern Cameroons had been annexed by the Republic of Cameroon. In his book *Les Blancs s'en Vont: Recits de Decolonization*, published in 1998 pp. 114-135, he concluded:

> To implement the results of the plebiscite, the governments of the Southern Cameroons and of the Cameroons met in a constitutional conference in Foumban, in the Bamoun country, familiar to both delegation on July 17, (1961). President Ahidjo from a position of strength submitted for debate a fake Federal draft constitution which had been carefully crafted by his French jurists. Ngu Foncha had no counter project. From a weak position, since the population which he represents does not exceed a quarter of that of French Cameroun, even in economic terms, Ngu Foncha accepted without discussion what was in effect an annexation. A joke was rife in Douala and Yaounde that the United Cameroon

was a bilingual francophone country.

The Republic of Cameroon's position of strength at Foumban drew also from the team of French jurists while Southern Cameroons' weak position was made worse by the absence of both the United Nations and the UK as Administering Authority whose presence should have made Foumban the International Conference which it was supposed to be. Both the United Nations and the British had backed down on the commitment made before the plebiscite to the Southern Cameroons electorate.

Double Talk: The view of the Republic of Cameroon before and after the annexation of the Southern Cameroons

Earlier, Mr. Ahmadou Ahidjo, as Prime Minister of the Republic of Cameroon (later President) told the 13th session of the United Nations in February 1959:

> I should not like the firmness and clarity of our stand to be interpreted as a desire for integration on my part which would sound the death knell to the hopes of our brothers in the zone under British Administration.
>
> We do not wish to bring the weight of our population to bear on our British brothers. We are not annexationists.
>
> In other words, if our brothers of the British zone wish to unite with an independent Cameroon, we are ready to discuss the matter with them, but we will discuss it on a footing of equality.

A few months after the Foumban bilateral talks, Ahidjo gave a policy speech at his party's Congress in Ebolowa in which he derided that very idea of equality in the UN plebiscite and precisely what he stood for in his speech at the United Nations on 25th of February 1959.

> The Cameroon Republic and the territory previously under British Trusteeship were on one side, an independent sovereign State possessing an international, legal personality, on the other, a territory without a political international status. It being unthinkable to tamper with the republican form of the regime, it was the Republic which had to transform itself into a federation, taking into account the return to it

of a part of its territory, a part possessing certain special characteristics. The question therefore was not that of the birth of a new Republic with a federal form. Owing to this logic, we decided therefore to amend the Constitution of the 21st of February 1960 since language and cultural differences needed to be given legal consideration. Thus, it was that at the historic Foumban Conference after a couple of days of work we announced the main outlines of the modification by which the Constitution of the 21st February 1960 should become the Constitution of the Federal Republic of Cameroon.

From this speech by President Ahidjo, it is clear that between Southern Cameroons and the Republic of Cameroon no "joining" as contemplated in the UN Plebiscite took place at all. According to Ahidjo, a part of their country was being returned to them by the UN and the UK. Secondly, in Foumban, Ahidjo took full advantage of the back out by the UN and UK, which abandoned the Southern Cameroons (still a dependency) mid-stream to set aside the envisaged Federal United Cameroon Republic of the UN plebiscite (which reflected the historical fact that the new Federation was a union of two independent States) to amend the Constitution of his country and name the new Federation as the Federal Republic of Cameroon. This was to emphasize that it was the Republic of Cameroon that had transformed itself into a Federation, and not the United Nations that had imposed Federation on the country, which they had formally rejected in their vote on Resolution 1608 XV. The Cameroon Federation therefore was, from the standpoint of Mr. Ahidjo and the Republic of Cameroon in mathematical terms not a 1+1 but a 1x1 with no need to write a new constitution or sign a Treaty of Union.

Falsification of World History in relation to Cameroon
According to the Republic of Cameroon, the decolonization of British Southern Cameroons was a return of part of their country long separated by colonial rule. It was the re-unification of what was German Kamerun before WWI. On Thursday 20th February 2014 therefore, the city of Buea hosted a celebration based on this revision of world history. Before arriving Buea for the celebration, President Biya rushed Prof. Jean Emmanuel Pondi to Addis Ababa to deliver a lecture on The Re-unification and Integration of Cameroon at the headquarters of the Africa Union.

The purpose of the UN Plebiscite in Southern Cameroons in 1961 was not to reconstitute German Kamerun nor had Southern Cameroons ever been part of French Cameroon (the Republic of Cameroon)! Under Article 119 of the Treaty of Versailles, Germany renounced all her rights and titles over her overseas possessions in favour of the Principle Allied and Associated powers that had defeated Germany in the war. The idea therefore of celebrating an event based on reconstituting German Kamerun seems absurd and ridiculous and may indeed be seen as a dishonest attempt to revise world history. Besides, no celebration of re-unification had ever taken place throughout the 53 previous years from 1961. It was a desperate event meant to glue-on false territorial claim.

Falsification of United Nations Decisions

According to the UN plebiscite Manifesto (*The Two Alternatives*) the official name of the Federation if the Southern Cameroons voted in the plebiscite to join La Republic du Cameroun was to be Federal United Cameroon Republic. At Foumban, Ahidjo not only imposed the Constitution of his country on Southern Cameroons, he gave the coming Federation a different name: Federal Republic of Cameroon. This was a major distortion. The *Federal United Cameroon Republic* proposed by the UN plebiscite was intended to reflect the historical fact that the two states of the Federation were separate states that "United" whereas the distorted name given by the Republic of Cameroon meant that the country was one single state that had adopted the federal system of government similar to the United States of America or Nigeria. The whole idea of "one and indivisible Cameroon" is underscored by this flawed reconstruction of world history.

Falsification of significant dates in the history of The Southern Cameroons.

In 1962 the government of the Southern Cameroons decided to commemorate 11th February each year as Plebiscite Day. The Republic of Cameroon came along and changed Southern Cameroons Plebiscite Day to Youth Day in order that more and more, the younger generations in Southern Cameroons would not know that the UN ever conducted a plebiscite on independence in their country and that after the plebiscite the world body "endorsed" the decisions of the people of Southern Cameroons to achieve independence. Similarly, the United Nations named 1st October as the date for terminating Trusteeship (which marked the start of Southern Cameroons independence). Yet, over the years the Republic of Cameroon came out in full force on 1st October with troops to harass the people of Southern Cameroons for marking the date of their independence. Often many are arrested, detained and tortured or killed. These arrests, detention, torture and killing have aimed at one thing: to wipe out any luster idea that the Southern Cameroons ever achieved independence.

The decision by the ruling CPDM political party in Cameroon to join the people of Southern Cameroons in celebrating 1st October in 2017 raised eyebrows. It had never happened before. On that first and only instance of doing that the CPDM was joining the people of Southern Cameroon to celebrate their independence day and no gun shot was heard East of the Mungo while in Southern Cameroons itself there was carnage and Mr. Biya and his Minister of Information were telling the world that they were fighting terrorists in the North West and South West Provinces! What a contradiction.

Southern Cameroons' Response to Republic of Cameroon's "One and Indivisible."

Southern Cameroons wishes the neighbouring Republic of Cameroon well with this idea. They do so in the hope that there are no delusions. When Southern Cameroons restores her statehood or asserts her right of self-determination and achieves international recognition of her sovereignty, no square inch of the territory of the Republic of Cameroon which achieved independence on 1st January 1960 would be reduced. The territory of that State remains the same as on the day and date of her independence. The restoration of Southern Cameroons statehood does not entail loss or dismemberment of any neighbouring state. Southern Cameroons' statehood restoration is not secession from the Republic of Cameroon because on 1st October 1961, (when Southern Cameroons achieved independence), her recognized international boundaries were in place. So, when the Republic of Cameroon talks of "one and indivisible Cameroon", it must be clear to all who listen that the territory referred to is the Republic of Cameroon which achieved independence on 1st January 1960. The challenge for the Republic of Cameroon since 1961 has been what to tell the world to justify her false territorial claim over the Southern Cameroons. Until she can successfully defend this legal basis before a court of law, the Republic of Cameroon's rhetoric on "one and indivisible Cameroon" has nothing to do with the separate state of the Southern Cameroons.

Her false claim and her falsification of Southern Cameroons history and at last her invasion of the state of Southern Cameroons will not win the people of Southern Cameroons into French Cameroon because facts do not cease to be facts just because they have been falsified. Mr. John

Cocoa was trying to make this point to Mr. James Coconut. His listener was not convinced. So, Mr. Cocoa said to his stubborn disputer, "Well, let's see now: How many legs does a cow have? The disgusted reply came back "Four of course." Mr. Cocoa agreed, "That's right. Now, suppose you call the cow's tail a leg, how many legs would the cow have?" His opponent replied confidently, "Why, five of course." Mr. Cocoa came back, "Now that's where you're wrong. Calling a cow's tail, a leg doesn't make it a leg."

In the same vein, the carnage in Southern Cameroons since 30th November 2017 under the pretext of fighting terrorism will not wipe the historical fact that the United Nations granted Southern Cameroons independence on 21st April 1961 to take effect from 1st October 1961 and Southern Cameroons' separate independence must be asserted.

Cameroon's Odd Revolution: Ahidjo's Coup

In all revolutions – at least the best known ones –it is the ordinary unhappy and those discontented with their lot who overthrow a government or a political system and carry out a replacement. For example in the American Revolution the war for independence was fought by the thirteen American colonies against Great Britain from 1775 - 1783. In the French revolution which started in 1789, it was the people that overthrew the French monarchy and this culminated in the empire of Napoleon I. In the Russian Revolution it was the conflict (1917- 1922) beginning in a Petrograd uprising on March 12, 1917 that resulted in a provisional moderate government and the abdication of Nicholas II, and eventually the Bolsheviks under Lenin overthrew this government (the October Revolution). The events in England between 1642 and 1689 brought about the execution of Charles I, the rise of the commonwealth, the dethronement of James II, and the establishment of a constitutional government under William III and Mary.

What Mr. Ahmadou Ahidjo did in Cameroon in May 1972 was not of the pattern of the overthrow and replacement of a government by those governed. It was a coup aimed specifically against the English-speaking state of the Southern Cameroons. He himself called it a revolution. If indeed it was, then it was an odd revolution from the known pattern.

FIGURE 3.5. Ahmadou Ahidjo, President of Cameroon (1960-1982)

On the 6th of May 1972 President Ahidjo went before the Cameroon National Assembly and announced his decision to change the federal structure to a unitary one. In his view the Federal Structure of the Cameroon state was a burden on the development of the country due to the functioning of three governments and four Legislative Assemblies. "The budget of the State of West Cameroon is still experiencing difficulties in spite of balancing subsidy from the Federation totaling more than 2000 million," Ahidjo said. Also, the people on both sides of the River Mungo needed to know each other better and learn to live together. He had accordingly decided to consult the people by way of a referendum on the institution of a unitary state, to be called the *United Republic of Cameroon*. Three days after this speech at the National Assembly (on 9th May 1972) President Ahidjo addressed the nation on the radio to introduce the draft Constitution for the United Republic of Cameroon. The new constitution stated that Cameroon was thenceforth one single State with one single government and one single assembly functioning according to simplified procedures, and the political regime was presidential.

On Saturday May 20th, 1972 voters were out at the polls to answer the question: "Do you approve, with a view to consolidating national unity and accelerating the economic social and cultural development of the nation, the draft constitution instituting a Republic, one and indivisible, to be styled the United Republic of Cameroon?" with a "YES" or "NO".

In the polling stations in the French speaking state of East Cameroon, however the ballot papers provided were "oui" or "yes" and as was to be expected Ahidjo scored 99% of the votes. Following the announcement of this overwhelming "majority" saying YES/OUI President Ahidjo for once was out on the streets of Yaounde on a triumphant walk visibly elated.

On June 2nd 1972 the new Unitary Constitution came into effect and on the 3rd of July the first government of the United Republic of Cameroon was formed of 28 members 8 of these being of Southern Cameroons origin. The two–star flag was quietly replaced by the one star one. President Ahidjo called this event "A peaceful Revolution" It was to call a spade, a spade a coup against the people of Southern Cameroons who had voted in the UN plebiscite to form a federation with the Republic of Cameroon (Article 1 of the Constitution of the Federal Republic of Cameroon). And by Article 47 of that Constitution the Federal character of the state was entrenched.

The Catapult Revolution

FIGURE 3.6. Catapult[2] improvised by Southern Cameroons youths and actually used by them for the defense of the homeland. Each catapult was operated by three fighters to hurl missiles at the attacking soldiers and even helicopters.

2   The catapult is believed to have been invented by Dionysius of Syracuse in 399 B.C. The one by three fighters were improvised by Southern Cameroons youths in Bamenda. Catapults were used in WWI by soldiers at the front to fling grenades and poisoned gas bombs at great distances.

What is generally referred to in Cameroon as the *Anglophone Problem* can be summarized from 3 standpoints:
1. Problems arising from the process of decolonization.
2. Problems arising from the policies of subjugation and integration.
3. Problems arising from marginalization.

So far in chapters 1, 2 and 3, these problems have been discussed. We will summarize them here in order to show the immediate causes and flashpoint of the 2017 catapult revolution and carnage that followed. First, the controversy as to whether there is such a thing as the Anglophone problem. A few ministers in the government of President Paul Biya claim that Anglophones in Cameroon have no problem. The most vocal of these being Mr. Atanga Nji Paul who was appointed Minister of Territorial Administration in 2018.

FIGURE 3.7. Atanga Nji Paul, Cameroon Minister of Territorial Administration

The Anglophone Problem
Central to the Cameroon Anglophone problem is the persistent exclusion of Anglophones from occupying senior positions in the Executive, Legislative, Judiciary and parastatals in Cameroon. However, let us start with the root cause of the problem; Let us start where the decolonization of BSC ended with the Administering Authority (the United Kingdom) surrendered, and subordinated the BSC (their own colony) to French Cameroon.

FIGURE 3.8. On November 21, 2016, Mancho Bibixy, a journalist for a local radio station in Bamenda, stood in an open casket and spoke to large crowds in Bamenda denouncing the social and economic marginalization of Anglophones in Cameroon indicating that he was prepared to die in protest against this marginalisation. This moment has been described as the beginning of the "Coffin Revolution" happening as it did in the context of an ongoing protest by Anglophone lawyers and teachers.

Problems arising from the process of decolonization
Departure from the Charter
The purpose of the International Trusteeship system and the process of decolonization are all clear in both the UN Charter and the Trusteeship Agreement but these were set aside and a controversial plebiscite conducted. The process of that plebiscite took away even the self-governing status that British Southern Cameroons had attained and finally both the UN and Administering Authority abandoned the plebiscite process unfinished. The main UN Resolution 1608 XV on the decolonization of British Cameroons was also abandoned unimplemented.

The experiment on "Independence by Joining "Failed"
The plebiscite on "Independence by Joining" was a violation of the UN charter and it failed when the Republic of Cameroon voted to reject UN proposal (in Resolution 1608 XV) that Southern Cameroons joins her. Although the plebiscite had been conducted the UN was unable to implement its outcome.

Cession and Annexation

As we have seen earlier in this essay when the Republic of Cameroon voted against Southern Cameroons joining her, the UN could not force Southern Cameroons to join her on the argument that the majority had voted for that proposal. Article 2:7 of the Charter forbids that. The UN could however have aborted that process of "independence by joining" and granted Southern Cameroons her independence by the process of the Charter and the Trusteeship Agreement. Instead, the UN pulled out of the process and left the Administering Authority to resolve the problem. The UK did this by transferring the Southern Cameroons to the Republic of Cameroon. Republic of Cameroon now accepted the "transfer" of the Southern Cameroons to her because this in effect was surrendering the territory to her and not the joining on terms of equal status.

Problems arising from the policies of subjugation and Assimilation

Issues arising from policies of assimilation include human rights violations against the people of Southern Cameroons.

> The subordination of the Southern Cameroons from the status of a self-governing to that of "Provinces" of the Republic of Cameroon contrary to agreements by the two states prior to the plebiscite.

> Suppression of the right of the people of Southern Cameroons on self-determination. The first three Prime Ministers of the Southern Cameroons were each elected by the people. The 4th however was appointed by the President of the Republic to replace Mr. Augustine N. Jua who had not finished his term of office via a democratic election by the people. He was replaced by S.T. Muna, a personal appointee of President Ahidjo.

FIGURE 3.9. Prime Minister Augustine N. Jua, third from left, was later replaced by Mr. S.T. Muna, first from left.

Frequent and unilateral revision of the constitution

This came along with the change of the name of the country without consulting (or involving) the people of Southern Cameroons or their leaders.

- From Federal United Cameroon Republic
- To: Federal Republic of Cameroon (with two-star flag)
- From: Federal Republic of Cameroon
- To: United Republic of Cameroon (with one-star flag)
- From: United Republic of Cameroon
- To: Republic of Cameroon (with one-star flag)

Relocating Economic Enterprises and Projects

Projects such as the Chad-Cameroon oil pipeline, and the construction of a deep-sea port and oil refinery were redirected to towns and cities in Francophone Cameroon thereby denying employment opportunities and secondary benefits to the people of Southern Cameroons.

Education:

- Understaffing of Primary Schools
- Schools frequently would be opened and located on political considerations and Parent Teachers Associations asked to employ and pay the teachers and build the needed classrooms.

Replacing City and Guilds Technical Examination with Certificat d'Aptitude Professional (CAP) and the BAC Technique

- This was preferred instead of investing in training English Speaking teachers of technical subjects.
- The transfer of Anglophones facing criminal charges from the South West and North West Provinces to Douala or Yaounde to be tried in French under the Napoleonic Code.
- The use and imposition of French, pidgin, "franglais" in educational institutions in the South West and North West Provinces as medium of instruction through French teachers who could not speak or write English. In their ruling in Communication 266/2003 handed down in 2009, the African Commission in Banjul told the Francophone-led and dominated government in Yaoundé to abolish "all discriminatory practices against the people of Northwest and Southwest Cameroon including equal usage of the English language in business transactions (215 (1)).

Problems Arising from the Marginalization of Anglophones

All the key positions in the executive branch of government, the legislature, the judiciary and parastatals are held by Francophones. All government ministries that handle big budgetary allocations are headed by Francophones. Minor ones like Culture, penitentiary and Audit where budgetary allocations lesser are assigned to the Anglophones. All professional training institutions in the country are headed by Francophones. The language of instruction in these institutions is French and entrance examination into them are in French

Flooding of government services in the South-West and North-West Regions with Francophone administrators (Governors, SDO's, DOs, Health workers in hospitals, Communication workers, magistrates, teachers, heads of services with staff who do not speak English and conduct their staff (and departmental meetings) in French. These are all the aspects of Anglophone problems in Cameroon.

In the course of the invasion of Southern Cameroons there was frequent deprivation of internet connection and social media from the English-speaking people of the two Anglophone Regions. In response to protests against the marginalization of Anglophones, the government shut down access to the internet in the two English-speaking provinces for 93 days between January and April 2017. The shutdown led Cameroonians unaffected by the ban to launch an online campaign with the hashtag #BringBackOurInternet to restore internet services to the Anglophone regions.

Strike by Common Law Lawyers and Teachers

In November 2016 several magistrates were posted by the government to Bamenda in the Northwest and to Buea in the Southwest. The newly appointed magistrates told lawyers in their jurisdictions to thenceforth make their submissions in French. The lawyers reminded the Francophone magistrates that they were in the English-speaking side of the country and the onus to work in English was theirs as was the responsibility to respect the Common Law tradition. The disagreement between the lawyers and the Francophone magistrates persisted and led to English-speaking lawyers petitioning the Minister of Justice and subsequently going on strike after the Minister ignored their petition.

A similar thing was happening at the universities in Bamenda and Buea where more and more Francophone teachers were sent to these institutions to teach. These teachers spoke no English and were teaching Anglophones students in French, pidgin or "franglais." The teachers petitioned the Minister of Higher Education and were similarly ignored, and they too decided to put down the chalk and all schools (from nursery, Primary, Secondary and Universities) in the Anglophone regions were shut down.

The population soon threw in their support behind both the striking teachers and lawyers pointing out how the Common Law tradition and the Anglo-Saxon education system were the first two important things in their colonial heritage that will not be compromised. The Francophone-led and dominated government in Yaoundé had stretched their hands for the last straw that broke the camel's back. If the two-state federation which British Southern Cameroons voted for in the UN plebiscite had not been abolished by French Cameroon, what was happening now would not be heard of at all.

In public primary schools, teachers were being ordered to teach French for which their training did not prepare them for. Teachers from all schools in Southern Cameroons (from nursery schools, primary, secondary and universities) started their own strike and all schools, colleges and universities were shut down. Both the Lawyers and teachers wrote petitions to their respective ministers stating their grievances and these petitions were ignored.

The government sent out ministers to Bamenda and Buea to order the reopening of schools. No agreement was reached between the Ministers on the one hand and lawyers and the teachers on the other hand. At several meetings between the government officials and these groups, the ministers kept insisting that schools should first reopen and the lawyers return to work before the grievances presented in the petitions of the two groups would be looked into.

FIGURE 3.10. Press coverage of the slaughter on 1st October 2017

In these negotiations it was frequently recalled that at the All Anglophone Conference (AAC1) held in Buea in April 1993 the English-speaking people of Southern Cameroons called for a return to the two state federation which they voted for in the UN plebiscite of February 1961 and that the government had done nothing about this since 1993. The lawyers and teachers met and formed an alliance- the Consortium which proposed the return to the two-state federation of 1961-1972 in Cameroon.

On the federation question, Southern Cameroonians were divided: The SDF Political party of Ni John Fru Ndi had been campaigning for a 4 state federation, The PAP party of Justice Paul Ayah for a 10 state federation and the Consortium of the Lawyers and teachers for a 2 state federation, and various nationalist groups (SCAPO, SCNC, Ambazonia, Youth League) etc. had been campaigning for de-annexation and the restoration of the Southern Cameroons statehood.

On 17 of January 2017 the leaders of the Consortium were arrested, carried to Yaoundé to be charged before a military tribunal. Justice Paul Ayah was arrested at his house in Yaoundé and detained in a separate location in Yaoundé. While under detention he was sent on retirement by the government.

The population of Southern Cameroonians responded with "Ghost towns" (deserted streets) once a week and on these days, streets were deserted, shops closed and of course schools were permanently closed.

For the celebration of 1st October 2017, the Cameroon government of President Biya mobilized the full force of the Cameroon army into towns and cities throughout Southern Cameroons with guns, grenades, tanks and helicopters equipped with guns. There was ruthless carnage and bloodbaths. People who had gone out carrying peace plants and green branches faced soldiers and guns of all sizes .

By evening, most Southern Cameroons streets were strewn with corpses. That Sunday, many who had been preparing for celebration found themselves under attack. Southern Cameroons youth bold and valiant, took the bull by the horns and showed a rare courage of their own conviction. Those of them who had finished High School and University and were now constrained to be self-employed as "okada" drivers, packed their bikes at home and turned to defense initiatives. While primary school children ran for catapults the ex-High School and University ones improvised bigger and stronger catapults operated by three fighters for the defense of their homeland.

On the 4th of September 2017 the Bishops of the Bamenda Provincial Episcopal Conference issued a declaration following the massive demonstrations and the curfew imposed on the North West and South West Regions from Friday, 29th September to Monday, 2nd October 2017. In the declaration they reiterated their earlier condemnation of violence.

PART IV

જે

DETERMINED TO BE FREE

Chapter 4

THE AFTERMATH OF CEDING

The events that shape history normally have causes and effects, before and afterwards respectively. The British introduced the idea of a plebiscite in the decolonization of British Southern Cameroons in the hope that the people of Southern Cameroons would choose to join the British colony of Nigeria and seal Anglo-Nigerian friendship but the results of the plebiscite did not go as the British had hoped.

Before the Plebiscite itself the UN Trusteeship Council wanted the constitutional arrangements for British Southern Cameroons joining Nigeria and for British Southern Cameroons joining French Cameroon to be made clear before the plebiscite itself. These arrangements were duly submitted by Nigeria and the Republic of Cameroon and published in THE TWO ALTERNATIVES. Nigeria sent in a detail and complete constitutional position while on the other hand Republic of Cameroon sent in a sketchy 2-page outline that was to be expanded later at the Post-Plebiscite Conference.

Nevertheless, these constitutional provisions for the future Federal United Cameroon Republic (as the future new country was going to be called) were clear. The new country was going to be a federation of sovereign States of **EQUAL status**. Page 4 of THE TWO ALTERNATIVES states:

> "A vote for attaining independence by joining the Republic would mean that, by an early date to be decided by the United Nations after consultations with the governments of the Southern Cameroons and the Cameroon Republic and the United Kingdom as Administering Authority, the Southern Cameroons and the Cameroon Republic would unite in a Federal United Cameroon Republic. The arrangements would be worked out after the plebiscite by a conference consisting of representative *delegations* of equal status from the Republic and the Southern Cameroons."

And page 15 carries the JOINT COMMUNIQUE which states under paragraph 2

> "(a) that immediately after the plebiscite and in the event of the people voting in favour of unification with the Cameroon Republic, a conference should be held attended by representatives of the Cameroon Republic and the Southern and Northern Cameroons.
>
> (b) that this conference, at which representatives of the Trusteeship Authority and possibly those of the United Nations would be present, would have as its aim the fixing of time limits and conditions for the transfer of **sovereign powers** to an organization representing the future Federation."

If the constitutional arrangement under the UN was **Equal Status** for joining Cameroon Republic then the December 2019 offer of a "Special Status" to the NW and SW Regions (as the British Southern Cameroons is under annexation referred to by the Cameroon Republic) raises the question as to why the people of British Southern Cameroons should accept a subordination (Cameroon Republic's "Special Status") in the place of the UN's **EQUAL status** and why they should accept this act of kneeling after the Cameroon Republic had carried up guns to attack the territorial integrity of the British Southern Cameroons and had slaughtered thousands on the shameless pretense that they were fighting terrorism. The people of Southern Cameroons have only one way to go that is left. That is **forward with the restoration** of the Statehood and independence of the Southern Cameroons.

The invasion and genocide aside it would be recalled that at the UN 994th plenary meeting of the General Assembly on April 21, 1961 Cameroon Republic voted against the independence of British Southern Cameroons and against BSC joining them which introduced an unexpected twist in the decolonization process for the British Southern Cameroons by which the United Nations could not force through the proposal of the British Southern Cameroons joining Cameroon Republic in violation of Article 2 (7) of the Charter. In the face of this embarrassing twist of events by Cameroon Republic the United Nations chose to back-out of the as yet unfinished plebiscite process and left the UK to resolve the impasse and the UK did this by transferring British Southern Cameroons to the President of the Republic of Cameroon in violation of UN GA Resolution 1514 XV and in utter disregard of the fact that

Cameroon Republic had voted against British Southern Cameroons joining the Cameroon Republic. This act of the Administering Authority coming after Cameroun Republic's vote against British Southern Cameroons joining them (as we have pointed out earlier in this essay) was irrefutably an act of surrendering or ceding the UN Trust Territory of British Southern Cameroons to Cameroon Republic and doing so precisely when the dawn of independence was showing over the mountains. .

In this part of the book we want to consider the consequences that followed in the wake of this unfortunate event of surrendering the Trust Territory of British Southern Cameroons. We will discuss three of these:

    a. Cameroon Republic's U-turn on Pre-Plebiscite Agreements with Southern Cameroons.
    b. Annexation and the occupation of the British Southern Cameroons.
    c. The policy of integration and Assimilation.

a) Cameroon Republic's U-turn on Pre-Plebiscite Agreements with Southern Cameroons

Cameroon Republic's u-turn on agreements with Southern Cameroons came swift on the heels of the ceding of British Southern Cameroons. What was immediately clear to Cameroon Republic following the act of ceding was that the idea in the Plebiscite arrangements on **Equality of the two States** in *the plebiscite arrangement was definitely off* the table. In his policy speech to the ruling UC Political Party in Ebolowa a few months after the Foumban Conference, President Ahmadou Ahidjo openly claimed that the idea of Equality of the two States was "unthinkable" British Southern Cameroons was in fact part of the territory of the Cameroon Republic that was being returned to her by the UN and the UK in 1961, a part having special characteristics concerning language and culture from the rest of the Mother Country (Cameroon). For that reason, at Foumban, they saw no reason for drawing a new Constitution. They had simply amended their country's existing Constitution to accommodate that part of their national territory that was being returned to them. This is how Ahidjo maneuvered the Foumban Conference to accomplish annexation.

However, annexation was achieved not only through Ahidjo's maneuvers. The instrument transferring the territory to the President of Cameroon Republic made no mention of any status which British Southern Cameroons was to enjoy after joining Cameroon Republic.

b) Annexation and the occupation of the British Southern Cameroons
The UK transfer of British Southern Cameroons to Cameroon Republic was a violation of Resolution 1514 XV, a menace to Southern Cameroons' independence and the excuse for annexation. The *Exchange of Notes on the Transfer of British Southern Cameroons to Cameroun Republic* (as the instrument is titled) smacks of international connivance when it is considered that both the United Kingdom and Cameroon Republic were members of the Committee set up by the General Assembly to work out detailed arrangements by which British Southern Cameroons was to join Cameroon Republic on October 1, 1961. However, two things are worth noting here: that Committee (Paragraph 5 of Resolution 1608 XV) was given its composition, terms of reference and deadline, but no mechanism for reporting back. Also, the Committee should have had a 4th even a 5th member bringing in neutral none-stake holders. As events turned out later it remains unclear what happened between the UK and the Cameroon Republic concerning the General Assembly Assignment in Paragraph 5 of Resolution 1608 XV. Nothing is heard of a report from that Committee and worse than that Resolution 1608 XV itself (which was duly adopted) has never been implemented.

The people of Southern Cameroons quite naturally did not readily connect the act of ceding with annexation. It was a matter of time for this awareness to be felt when discrimination and marginalization raised their heads in full view and as heat raised the temperature of annexation higher and higher both sides talked of the need for peace with Cameroon Republic emphasizing national unity and the Constitutionality of a "one and indivisible Cameroon" which was understood to mean *peace with annexation.* On their part, the people of Southern Cameroons called for examining the root causes of the problem, in particular the basis of Cameroon Republic's territorial claim on Southern Cameroons in other words, *peace with justice.* Southern Cameroons challenged the Cameroon Republic to publish any legal instrument in its possession by which she was laying claim to the territory of British Southern Cameroons.

c) The policy of integration and Assimilation
This policy was undertaken as prelude to abolishing Federalism in Cameroon and introducing the Unitary State. President Ahidjo's declaration before the 13th Session of the United Nations in February 1959 that his country had no desire of ever integrating the people of the British Southern Cameroons and that if the people of Southern Cameroons wished to join the Cameroon Republic they would discuss the matter on a footing of equality was a calculated allurement and a snare

to attract the people of Southern Cameroons to *come on*. The policy of integration was to be undertaken by Ahidjo himself camouflaged as the ***movement for national unity***. After testing the ground for a while on the process of national unity, Ahidjo went before the National Assembly on May 6 1972 and declared that he had decided to conduct a referendum for instituting the Unitary State in Cameroon.

Ahidjo justified the need for changing the Federal form of State to a unitary one: the functioning of three governments and four Assemblies was expensive and exhausted resources that otherwise should have been used in the economic, social and cultural development. Once the unitary state was in place, the process of integration was accelerated. The discrimination and marginalization of Anglophones intensified and the people of Southern Cameroons and whatever problems they had, was spoken of as the same minority problems that other ethnic groups in Cameroon were experiencing. Resentment and resistance smoldered and manifested in street action and strikes. Cameroon Republic finally picked up guns and declared war to enforce a "one and indivisible Cameroon" through military conquest.

Perspectives of the Conflict

The Anglophones' demand for return to Federalism is ignored

The All Anglophones Conference (AAC I) held at Mount Mary on April 2, 1993 marked the awakening of Southern Cameroons nationalism. Over five thousand Anglophones (Political Leaders, Members of Parliament, Natural Rulers, Opinion Leaders, etc.,) came together to make their contribution in the context of President Biya's call for Constitutional reform. The Conference called for a return to the two State Federation for which the Southern Cameroons voted for as basis for joining the Republic of Cameroon. The Conference also charted the direction and peaceful approach of the struggle for de-Annexation and self-determination and adopted the Motto: *The force of Argument; not the argument of Force.*

President Paul Biya apparently turned a deaf ear on the recommendations of the Anglophones. The following year the Anglophones held a second AAC II in the city of Bamenda and decided that if President Biya persisted to ignore their call for a return to the Federal system which was the basis on which the people of British Southern Cameroons came into political association with the Republic of Cameroon, Southern Cameroons would take steps to restore its statehood and separate independence and not call a further Anglophone Conference. The declaration of the Restoration of statehood and independence by Dr. Ayuk Tabe on October 1, 2017 was an implementation of the AAC II Proclamation in Bamenda and the follow up Conclave consultations in Lagos, Nigeria.

As tension rose between Francophones and Anglophones in the Cameroons, the UN Secretary General Antonio Guterres was in Yaoundé on October 27, 2017 and held a four-hour meeting with President Paul Biya. As always Biya convinced Guterres that he was addressing the Anglophone Question and things were returning to normal. This is the standard pattern that Biya has used to buy time for his rule over the years. The UN Secretary General returned to New York with the false and deceptive assurance from Cameroon that things were normalizing between the two States in Cameroon. Mr. Antonio Guterres's visit to Yaoundé was seen as an attempt to prevent the tension in Cameroon from flaring into violence. This was too little too late. Why do we say so?

The United Nations was founded to maintain international peace and security. The scope of maintaining that international peace and security includes preventing conflicts before they start and creating conditions to permit peace to flourish. The golden principle that *prevention is better than cure* is readily understood in matters of health. Could what was unfolding in British Southern Cameroons have been prevented? For over five decades British Southern Cameroons had sent petition after petition to the UN about their own decolonization which was abandoned unfinished. They pointed out how without the implementation of UN GA Resolution 1608 XV and UN GA Resolution 1514 XV and without a Treaty of Union between the two States no Union had been established between the Republic of Cameroon and the British Southern Cameroons. British Southern Cameroons (its territory and people) had simply been transferred and subordinated to the other partner in a federation of States of Equal Status contrary to written agreement in the plebiscite arrangements. The United Nations heard all these and remained silent – for silence never commits any diplomatic blunders.

Without the implementation of Resolutions 1608 (XV) and the landmark Res. 1514, no decolonization and no union with Republic of Cameroon were achieved.

Fuel on the Fire: The Church dances Crabwise

As elsewhere in Africa, the Christian missionaries to Southern Cameroons built churches, schools and hospitals to continue the ministry of the Lord Jesus Christ (here on earth). He preached the Good News, taught and healed the sick. In the wake of the Southern Cameroons Common Law Lawyers' and teachers' strike, the government of President

Biya ordered the churches to disassociate themselves from the strike action by reopening their own mission schools.

The initial response by the Churches was that they did not call for the strike and were not therefore the ones to call it off. The government decided to send in troops into Southern Cameroons and to also arrest the leaders of the Consortium. A reign of terror spread throughout Southern Cameroons following the arrival of the armed forces characterized by brutality, torture and killing of unarmed Southern Cameroonians. Soldiers dragged students from university hostels and forced them to roll in (and drink from) sewage. Girls were raped, some detained and others transported to unknown destinations.

The Churches sent a joint memorandum to the government urging it to handle the crisis peacefully without resorting to violence, but the brutalities, arrests and killings only intensified. The Catholic Church in their Cameroon Panorama of January 2017 put out a detailed analysis of the crisis and made suggestions for resolving the situation peacefully. The government instead intensified the violence by sending armed troops to all towns and cities of Southern Cameroons ostensibly to "restore order". They ordered a disconnection of the internet and social media throughout Southern Cameroons several times.

In response, Southern Cameroons groups working for the restoration of Southern Cameroons statehood from different parts of the world (at home, South Africa, USA and Europe) met in Lagos Nigeria and decided to sink their differences and come together under a united front called SCACUF (Southern Cameroons Consortium United Front) in February 2017. Nine groups were invited from the home front, South Africa, USA and Europe. Seven of the nine groups attended the gathering. The two that were unable to attend, arranged to address the gathering from their different locations/headquarters associating their organizations with the decisions of the meeting. The group elected a University lecturer Dr. Julius Ayuk Tabe as leader of the United Front and interim Chairman of the Southern Cameroons Executive Council (called "Governing Council" for the interim duration).

Meanwhile the heads of three of the oldest Christian denominations in Southern Cameroons (The Baptists, the Presbyterians and the Catholic Churches) received court summons to appear in court in either Buea or Bamenda. The summons served on April 12, 2017 by a bailiff was reportedly from a consortium of parents seeking 150 billion francs CFA in damages over the non-opening of mission schools. Before the date for the court appearance of the priests, pastors and bishops the people whose names were on the court summons as plaintiffs/complainants made public declarations disclaiming the use of their names as complainants against the Churches.

On the day of the hearing the court premises in Buea and Bamenda were swamped by Christians, pastors and priests from all corners of the Southern Cameroons. The case was adjourned but the event and pictures were headlines on the front pages of Southern Cameroons newspapers and newspapers in French speaking Cameroon throughout the week. This made matters worse for the Government and strengthened the determination of the leaders of the Southern Cameroons. Many in Southern Cameroons thanked the church recalling that though the church is apolitical they cannot be neutral in a situation of unjust oppression. The place of the Church would always be with the oppressed and not with the oppressor.

The position of the Church with the oppressed people of the Southern Cameroons was to be expected. Earlier on the Fiftieth Anniversary of the United Nations, Pope John Paul II had reminded the world body that "a presupposition of a nation's right is certainly its right to exist; therefore no one - neither a state nor another nation nor an international organization is ever justified in asserting that an individual nation is not worthy of existence." This statement by the Holy Father seemed to have been conceived with the Southern Cameroons in mind. The initial reaction from the church seems to draw inspiration from this statement by the Pope.

In July 2017, after Parent Teacher Associations (PTAs) of the Bamenda Ecclesiastical Province called for an end to the school boycott, Anglophone Bishops ordered school administrators to begin registration of pupils and students for the 2017/2018 academic year. With this u-turn, the churches started campaigning for schools to resume. Radio stations owned by Christian churches were engaged in the campaign for schools to reopen. However, allegations filtered out in the social media that after weeks of intense government consultations with church leaders behind closed doors, the churches had been given large sums of money as subventions and requested to take sides with the government.

The Southern Cameroons Governing Council called for a nationwide peaceful protest on 22 September 2017. The response was massive throughout Southern Cameroons and everywhere the police and gendarmerie were overwhelmed by the sheer numbers that turned out carrying peace plants and green branches (well recognized symbols of peace). The overwhelming participation by Southern Cameroonians on 22 September 2017 everywhere throughout the territory caught the Cameroon government in Yaoundé by surprise and left them completely dumbfounded. That was perhaps why they swung to the other extreme on 1st October 2017.

Strike by Common Law Lawyers and Teachers

In November 2016, several magistrates were posted by the government to Bamenda in the Northwest and to Buea in the Southwest. The newly appointed magistrates told lawyers in these jurisdictions to thenceforth make their submissions in French. The lawyers reminded the Francophone magistrates that they were in the English-speaking side of the country and the onus to work in English was theirs as was the responsibility to respect the Common Law tradition. The disagreement between the lawyers and the Francophone magistrates persisted and led to English-speaking lawyers petitioning the Minister of Justice and subsequently going on strike after the Minister ignored their petition.

A similar thing was happening at the universities in Bamenda and Buea where more and more Francophone teachers were sent to these institutions to teach. These teachers spoke no English and were teaching Anglophones students in French, pidgin or "franglais." The teachers petitioned the Minister of Higher Education and were similarly ignored, and they too decided to put down the chalk and all schools (from nursery, Primary, Secondary and Universities) in the Anglophone regions were shut down.

The population soon threw in their support behind both the striking teachers and lawyers pointing out how the Common Law tradition and the Anglo-Saxon education system were the first two important things in their colonial heritage that will not be compromised. The Francophonc-led and dominated government in Yaoundé had stretched their hands for the last straw that broke the camel's back. If the two-state federation which British Cameroons voted for in the UN plebiscite had not been abolished by French Cameroon what was happening now would not be heard of at all.

In public primary schools, teachers were being ordered to teach French for which their training did not prepare them for. Teachers from all schools in Southern Cameroons (from nursery schools, primary, secondary and universities) started their own strike and all schools, colleges and universities were shut down. Both the Lawyers and teachers wrote petitions to their respective ministers stating their grievances and these petitions were ignored.

The government in Yaoundé sent out ministers to Bamenda and Buea to order the reopening of schools. No agreement was reached between the Ministers on the one hand and lawyers and the teachers on the other hand. At several meetings between the government officials and these groups, the ministers kept insisting that schools should first reopen and the lawyers return to work before the grievances presented in the petitions of the two groups would be looked into.

In these negotiations it was frequently recalled that at the All Anglophone Conference (AAC1) held in Buea in April 1993, the English-speaking people of Southern Cameroons called for a return to the two state federation which they voted for in the UN plebiscite of February 1961 and that the government had done nothing about this since 1993. The lawyers and teachers met and formed an alliance: the Consortium which proposed the return to the two-state federation of 1961-1972 in Cameroon.

On the federation question, Southern Cameroonians were divided: The SDF of Ni John Fru Ndi had been campaigning for a four-state federation. The PAP party of Justice Paul Ayah for a 10 state federation and the Consortium of the Lawyers and teachers for a two-state federation, and various nationalist groups (SCAPO, SCNC, Ambazonia, Youth League) etc. had been campaigning for de-annexation and the restoration of the Southern Cameroons statehood.

On 17 of January 2017 the leaders of the Consortium were arrested, carried to Yaoundé to be charged before a military tribunal. Justice Paul Ayah was arrested at his house in Yaoundé and detained in a separate location in Yaoundé. While under detention he was sent on retirement by the government.

The population of Southern Cameroonians responded with "Ghost towns" (deserted streets) once a week and on these days, streets were deserted, shops closed and of course schools were permanently closed.

CONCLUDING REFLECTIONS

God Saw Goodness in Separation

In his creation (Genesis 1) God separated light from darkness. He called the light "day" and the darkness "night." He saw that what He had created was good. He created a vast expanse to separate the water under the expanse from the water above it. He separated land and the seas and He saw goodness in separating what he brought into being. He lighted the vast expanse above to distinctly separate the day from the night with lights and He saw that what He brought forth and separated was good indeed. On January 1993 the nation of Czechoslovakia separated peacefully into Czech Republic and Slovakia and Europe did not melt or disintegrate. In many wars of independence colonies have fought with bitterness with colonial masters and once separation and independence was achieved the fighting parties have become good friends again. An example today is the United States and the UK that are best friends after the war of 1812. In the conflict in Cameroon the people of Southern Cameroons did not start the fighting. The Southern Cameroons youths picked up stones and catapults to defend themselves and their homeland. After three years the conflict is shaping out to be a re-enactment of David and Goliath. Republic of Cameroon has proposed special status and decentralization: too little; too late. Decentralization in Cameroon is practically one way of recentralizing power to the central government. In any case, Southern Cameroons has nothing for or against the domestic affairs of a neighbouring country. Southern Cameroons has crossed the Rubicon.

In September 1995 the people of Southern Cameroons conducted a Signature Referendum in Southern Cameroons. The question put to the electorate in that referendum was: Do you want the Southern Cameroons to achieve full independence by peaceful separation from La Republique du Cameroun? The official report of this referendum presented to the United Nations showed that 99% of the people of Southern Cameroons were in favour of separation from La Republique du Cameroun and restoring their full independence.

Since making this decision in a referendum and reporting to the United Nations, the people of Southern Cameroons have not relented efforts to restore their statehood and independence peacefully. Indeed since 1961 when the process of the decolonization of the UN Trust Territory of the British Southern Cameroons ended up ironically in the cession and annexation of the Territory, the Republic of Cameroon has claimed (and insisted) that the Southern Cameroons is a part of their country that was returned to her by the United Kingdom and the United Nations in 1961 and therefore that any attempt by Southern Cameroons to separate amounted to secession which must be stopped with guns which introduced the argument of force. Republic of Cameroon has been assured that in the conflict they initiated "the force of argument" will triumph.

The year 2017 witnessed the escalation of hostilities between the two states. On 22nd September 2017 there was nationwide demonstrations called by the United Front of all Southern Cameroons groups working for the restoration of the statehood and independence of the Southern Cameroons. The massive turnout on that date while asserting the determination of the people of Southern Cameroons for independence took the government of the Republic of Cameroon by complete surprise on something they had underestimated and sought to minimize all along. Nine days later, on 1st October, the Republic of Cameroon mobilized its army and Air Force with tanks and helicopters into Southern Cameroons and there was blood bath. Peaceful demonstrators were killed all over Southern Cameroons Men and youths were forced to dig mass graves at gun point and the supervising soldiers then shot and killed all those digging and dragged other corpses from the streets and heaped them in the mass graves before covering.

"Is this Los Angeles?"

On May 20, 1927, Charles Lindbergh took off in the Spirit of St. Louis from New York and arrived in France 33 hours later, completing the first nonstop flight alone over the Atlantic. Eleven years later in 1938 another US citizen by name Douglas Corrigan took off alone in his own plane from Brooklyn, New York on an announced flight to Long Beach California. After a twenty-three-hour flight he touched down in Dublin, Ireland, and his first words to officials there were. "Is this Los Angeles? For years after this event, people laughed at this miscalculation, and Douglas Corrigan came to be called "wrong-way Corrigan" for flying in the opposite direction.

The story of British Southern Cameroons after World War II is like that of "Wrong-Way Corrigan." Under the UN (and supervised by the Trusteeship Council so that nothing should go wrong) British Southern

Cameroons took off on the journey of decolonization to freedom. She landed in the desert of political servitude with a colonial yoke of a third world country. The Agreement on Equal Status of sovereign states if she voted to join the Republic after the twists and turns to be different: the offer of a *special status* which she was expected to kneel for it as favour from the other partner (of equal status in the Union who was being considerate enough to consider Southern Cameroons for promotion from the status of two Provinces to *special status*).

In 1963 Corrigan admitted that his trip across the Atlantic had really been planned. Unable to get clearance to cross the ocean, he went ahead and made the flight "by mistake" i.e. on purpose.

The story of the ceding of the British Southern Cameroons to the Republic of Cameroon does not veil the fact that this was planned deliberately. If it were not so, we would be forced to ask questions that may either be childish or childlike: How was France (another European colonial power of the era) able to bring all her own UN Trust Territories in West Africa to independence while the British failed to do so with all of her own? Was the decision by Britain that British Trust Territories in West Africa should join their neighbouring British colonies from British inability to accomplish what France accomplished without attaching theirs to neighbouring French colonies?

Flowers that Bloom in Paradise

If (like the present writer) you find these questions childlike, (not childish), then don't blame Sir James Robertson, the Governor General who in defending the indefensible while in Buea raised matters of injustice and justification. The people of Southern Cameroons have not blamed those who spent years, resources and efforts steering the ship of their homeland on a long circuitous journey only to finally land them somewhere in the middle of nowhere - all in the inglorious name of decolonization. They have instead concentrated on ending the longest colonial rule on the continent of Africa and getting the forces of occupation from Republic of Cameroon to get out of their homeland. The bloody atrocities and barbaric killings from Mr. Biya's ruthless forces were bitter experiences for the armless people of Southern Cameroons but they remained determined to be free and undaunted. Many of them died with their boots on and clasping their crude catapults. They died as heroes of their homeland. Mr. Ian McLaren commenting on the highest joy of a Christian said, "No flower blooms in paradise that was not transplanted from Gethsemane."

When you look on the bright side,
you're acknowledging that there is a
dark side at which you are choosing
not to gaze. If you think that the
darkest hour is before the dawn
you accept that you are moving
from darkness into light.

Srikumar Rao

Denver, Colorado USA
Thursday 16 January 2020

BRITISH MANDATE FOR THE CAMEROONS [1]

The Council of the League of Nations:

Whereas, by Article 119 of the treaty of peace with Germany signed at Versailles on June 28, 1919, Germany renounced in favor of the Principal Allied and Associated Powers all her rights over her oversea possessions, including therein the Cameroons; and

Whereas the Principal Allied and Associated Powers agreed that the Governments of France and Great Britain should make a joint recommendation to the League of Nations as to the future of the said territory; and

Whereas the Governments of France and Great Britain have made a joint recommendation to the Council of the League of Nations that a mandate to administer in accordance with Article 22 of the Covenant of the League of Nations that part of the Cameroons lying to the west of the line agreed upon in the declaration of July 10, 1919, annexed hereto, referred to in Article 1, should be conferred upon His Britannic Majesty; and

Whereas the Governments of France and Great Britain have proposed that the mandate should be formulated in the following terms; and

Whereas His Britannic Majesty has agreed to accept the mandate in respect of the said territory, and has undertaken to exercise it on behalf of the League of Nations in accordance with the following provisions;

Confirming the said mandate, defines its terms as follows:

ARTICLE 1

The territory for which a mandate is conferred upon His Britannic Majesty comprises that part of the Cameroons which lies to the west of the line laid down in the declaration signed on July 10, 1919, of which a copy is annexed hereto.

This line may, however, be slightly modified by mutual agreement between His Britannic Majesty's Government and the Government of the French Republic where an examination of the localities shows that it is undesirable, either in the interests of the inhabitants or by reason of any inaccuracies in the map, Moisel 1: 300,000, annexed to the declaration, to adhere strictly to the line laid down therein.

The delimitation on the spot of this line shall be carried out in accordance with the provisions of the said declaration.

The final report of the mixed commission shall give the exact description of the boundary line as traced on the spot; maps signed by the commissioners shall be annexed to the report. This report with its annexes shall be drawn up in triplicate: one of these shall be deposited in the archives of the League of Nations, one shall be kept by His Britannic Majesty's Government, and one by the Government of the French Republic.

[1] *League of Nations Official Journal*, Aug. 1922, p. 869.

ARTICLE 2

The Mandatory shall be responsible for the peace, order and good government of the territory, and for the promotion to the utmost of the material and moral well-being and the social progress of its inhabitants.

ARTICLE 3

The Mandatory shall not establish in the territory any military or naval bases, nor erect any fortifications, nor organize any native military force except for local police purposes and for the defence of the territory.

ARTICLE 4

The Mandatory:

(1) shall provide for the eventual emancipation of all slaves, and for as speedy an elimination of domestic and other slavery as social conditions will allow:

(2) shall suppress all forms of slave trade;

(3) shall prohibit all forms of forced or compulsory labor, except for essential public works and services, and then only in return for adequate remuneration;

(4) shall protect the natives from abuse and measures of fraud and force by the careful supervision of labor contracts and the recruiting of labor;

(5) shall exercise a strict control over the traffic in arms and ammunition and the sale of spirituous liquors.

ARTICLE 5

In the framing of laws relating to the holding or transfer of land, the Mandatory shall take into consideration native laws and customs, and shall respect the rights and safeguard the interests of the native population.

No native land may be transferred, except between natives, without the previous consent of the public authorities, and no real rights over native land in favor of non-natives may be created except with the same consent.

The Mandatory shall promulgate strict regulations against usury.

ARTICLE 6

The Mandatory shall secure to all nationals of states members of the League of Nations the same rights as are enjoyed in the territory by his own nationals in respect of entry into and residence in the territory, the protection afforded to their person and property, and acquisition of property, movable and immovable, and the exercise of their profession or trade, subject only to the requirements of public order, and on condition of compliance with the local law.

Further, the Mandatory shall ensure to all nationals of states members of the League of Nations on the same footing as to his own nationals, freedom of transit and navigation, and complete economic, commercial and industrial equality; except that the Mandatory shall be free to organize essential public works and services on such terms and conditions as he thinks just.

Concessions for the development of the natural resources of the territory shall be granted by the Mandatory without distinction on grounds of nationality between the nationals of all states members of the League of Nations, but on such conditions as will maintain intact the authority of the local government.

Concessions having the character of a general monopoly shall not be granted. This provision does not affect the right of the Mandatory to create monopolies of a purely fiscal character in the interest of the territory under mandate and in order to provide the territory with fiscal resources which seem best suited to the local requirements; or, in certain cases, to carry out the development of natural resources, either directly by the state or by a controlled agency, provided that there shall result therefrom no monopoly of the natural resources for the benefit of the Mandatory or his nationals, directly or indirectly, nor any preferential advantage which shall be inconsistent with the economic, commercial and industrial equality hereinbefore guaranteed.

The rights conferred by this article extend equally to companies and associations organized in accordance with the law of any of the members of the League of Nations, subject only to the requirements of public order, and on condition of compliance with the local law.

ARTICLE 7

The Mandatory shall ensure in the territory complete freedom of conscience and the free exercise of all forms of worship which are consonant with public order and morality; missionaries who are nationals of states members of the League of Nations shall be free to enter the territory and to travel and reside therein, to acquire and possess property, to erect religious buildings and to open schools throughout the territory; it being understood, however, that the Mandatory shall have the right to exercise such control as may be necessary for the maintenance of public order and good government, and to take all measures required for such control.

ARTICLE 8

The Mandatory shall apply to the territory any general international conventions applicable to his contiguous territory.

ARTICLE 9

The Mandatory shall have full powers of administration and legislation in the area subject to the mandate. This area shall be administered in accordance with the laws of the Mandatory as an integral part of his territory and subject to the above provisions.

The Mandatory shall therefore be at liberty to apply his laws to the territory under the mandate subject to the modifications required by local conditions, and to constitute the territory into a customs, fiscal or administrative union or federation with the adjacent territories under his sovereignty or control, provided always that the measures adopted to that end do not infringe the provisions of this mandate.

ARTICLE 10

The Mandatory shall make to the Council of the League of Nations an annual report to the satisfaction of the Council, containing full information concerning the measures taken to apply the provisions of this mandate.

ARTICLE 11

The consent of the Council of the League of Nations is required for any modification of the terms of this mandate.

ARTICLE 12

The Mandatory agrees that, if any dispute whatever should arise between the Mandatory and another member of the League of Nations relating to the interpretation or the application of the provisions of the mandate, such dispute, if it cannot be settled by negotiation, shall be submitted to the Permanent Court of International Justice provided for by Article 14 of the Covenant of the League of Nations.

The present instrument shall be deposited in original in the archives of the League of Nations. Certified copies shall be forwarded by the Secretary-General of the League of Nations to all members of the League.

Done at London, the twentieth day of July one thousand nine hundred and twenty-two.

CAMEROONS—FRANCO-BRITISH DECLARATION [1]

The undersigned:

Viscount Milner, Secretary of State for the Colonies of the British Empire.

M. Henry Simon, Minister for the Colonies of the French Republic, have agreed to determine the frontier, separating the territories of the Cameroons, placed respectively under the authority of their governments, as it is traced on the map, Moisel 1: 300,000 annexed to the present declaration,[2] and defined in the description in three articles also annexed hereto.

(Signed)   MILNER.
HENRY SIMON.

London, July 10, 1919.

[1] *League of Nations Official Journal*, Aug. 1922, p. 872.
[2] The original 1: 300,000 map is attached to the signed declaration.

No. 118

———

TRUSTEESHIP AGREEMENT FOR THE TERRITORY OF THE CAMEROONS UNDER BRITISH ADMINISTRATION

Approved by the General Assembly of the United Nations on 13 December 1946

English and French official texts. The registration ex officio *by the Secretariat of the United Nations took place on 1 October 1947.*

———

ACCORD DE TUTELLE POUR LE TERRITOIRE DU CAMEROUN SOUS ADMINISTRATION BRITANNIQUE

Approuvé par l'Assemblée générale des Nations Unies le 13 décembre 1946

Textes officiels anglais et français. L'enregistrement d'office par le Secrétariat de l'Organisation des Nations Unies a eu lieu le 1er octobre 1947.

No. 118. TRUSTEESHIP AGREEMENT[1] FOR THE TERRI-
TORY OF THE CAMEROONS UNDER BRITISH ADMIN-
ISTRATION, APPROVED BY THE GENERAL ASSEMBLY
OF THE UNITED NATIONS ON 13 DECEMBER 1946

Whereas the Territory known as the Cameroons under British Mandate[2]
and hereinafter referred to as the Territory has been administered in accordance
with Article 22 of the Covenant of the League of Nations under a mandate conferred on His Britannic Majesty; and

Whereas Article 75[3] of the United Nations Charter, signed at San Francisco
on 26 June 1945, provides for the establishment of an International Trusteeship
System for the administration and supervision of such territories as may be placed
thereunder by subsequent individual agreements; and

Whereas, under Article 77 of the said Charter, the International Trusteeship
System may be applied to territories now held under mandate; and

Whereas His Majesty has indicated his desire to place the Territory under
the said International Trusteeship System; and

Whereas, in accordance with Articles 75 and 77 of the said Charter, the plac-
ing of a territory under the International Trusteeship System is to be effected
by means of a trusteeship agreement,

Now, therefore, the General Assembly of the United Nations hereby resolves
to approve the following terms of Trusteeship for the Territory:

Article 1

The Territory to which this Agreement applies comprises that part of the
Cameroons lying to the west of the boundary defined by the Franco-British Decla-
ration of 10 July 1919,[4] and more exactly defined in the Declaration made by
the Governor of the Colony and Protectorate of Nigeria and the Governor of the
Cameroons under French mandate which was confirmed by the exchange of
Notes between His Majesty's Government in the United Kingdom and the French
Government of 9 January 1931.[5] This line may, however, be slightly modified by

---

[1] Came into force on 13 December 1946, date of approval of the Agreement by the General
Assembly of the United Nations (resolution 63 (I)).
[2] League of Nations, *Official Journal,* Volume 2 (1922), pages 869 to 871.
[3] For references to Articles 75 to 91 of the United Nations Charter, see pages 80 to 88
of this Volume.
[4] *British and Foreign State Papers,* Volume 118, page 887.
[5] *British and Foreign State Papers,* Volume 134, page 238.

mutual agreement between His Majesty's Government in the United Kingdom and the Government of the French Republic where an examination of the localities shows that it is desirable in the interests of the inhabitants.

Article 2

His Majesty is hereby designated as Administering Authority for the Territory, the responsibility of the administration of which will be undertaken by His Majesty's Government in the United Kingdom of Great Britain and Northern Ireland.

Article 3

The Administering Authority undertakes to administer the Territory in such a manner as to achieve the basic objectives of the International Trusteeship System laid down in Article 76 of the United Nations Charter. The Administering Authority further undertakes to collaborate fully with the General Assembly of the United Nations and the Trusteeship Council in the discharge of all their functions as defined in Article 87 of the United Nations Charter, and to facilitate any periodic visits to the Territory which they may deem necessary, at times to be agreed upon with the Administering Authority.

Article 4

The Administering Authority shall be responsible: (a) for the peace, order, good government and defence of the Territory and (b) for ensuring that it shall play its part in the maintenance of international peace and security.

Article 5

For the above-mentioned purposes and for all purposes of this Agreement, as may be necessary, the Administering Authority:

(a) Shall have full powers of legislation, administration and jurisdiction in the Territory and shall administer it in accordance with the authority's own laws as an integral part of its territory with such modification as may be required by local conditions and subject to the provisions of the United Nations Charter and of this Agreement;

(b) Shall be entitled to constitute the Territory into a customs, fiscal or administrative union or federation with adjacent territories under its sovereignty or control, and to establish common services between such territories and the Territory where such measures are not inconsistent with the basic objectives of the International Trusteeship System and with the terms of this Agreement;

(c) And shall be entitled to establish naval, military and air bases, to erect fortifications, to station and employ its own forces in the Territory and to take all such other measures as are in its opinion necessary for the defence of the Territory and for ensuring that it plays its part in the maintenance of international peace and security. To this end the Administering Authority may make use of volunteer forces, facilities and assistance from the Territory in carrying out the obligations towards the Security Council undertaken in this regard by the Administering Authority, as well as for local defence and the maintenance of law and order within the Territory.

Article 6

The Administering Authority shall promote the development of free political institutions suited to the Territory. To this end the Administering Authority shall assure to the inhabitants of the Territory a progressively increasing share in the administrative and other services of the Territory; shall develop the participation of the inhabitants of the Territory in advisory and legislative bodies and in the government of the Territory, both central and local, as may be appropriate to the particular circumstances of the Territory and its people; and shall take all other appropriate measures with a view to the political advancement of the inhabitants of the Territory in accordance with Article 76 b of the United Nations Charter. In considering the measures to be taken under this article the Administering Authority shall, in the interests of the inhabitants, have special regard to the provisions of article 5 (a) of this Agreement.

Article 7

The Administering Authority undertakes to apply in the Territory the provisions of any international conventions and recommendations already existing or hereafter drawn up by the United Nations or by the specialized agencies referred to in Article 57 of the Charter, which may be appropriate to the particular circumstances of the Territory and which would conduce to the achievement of the basic objectives of the International Trusteeship System.

Article 8

In framing laws relating to the holding or transfer of land and natural resources, the Administering Authority shall take into consideration native laws and customs, and shall respect the rights and safeguard the interests, both present and future, of the native population. No native land or natural resources may be transferred except between natives, save with the previous consent of the

No. 118

competent public authority. No real rights over native land or natural resources in favour of non-natives may be created except with the same consent.

Article 9

Subject to the provisions of article 10 of this Agreement, the Administering Authority shall take all necessary steps to ensure equal treatment in social, economic, industrial and commercial matters for all Members of the United Nations and their nationals and to this end:

(*a*) Shall ensure the same rights to all nationals of Members of the United Nations as to its own nationals in respect of entry into and residence in the Territory, freedom of transit and navigation, including freedom of transit and navigation by air, acquisition of property both movable and immovable, the protection of persons and property and the exercise of professions and trades;

(*b*) Shall not discriminate on grounds of nationality against nationals of any Member of the United Nations in matters relating to the grant of concessions for the development of the natural resources of the Territory, and shall not grant concessions having the character of a general monopoly;

(*c*) Shall ensure equal treatment in the administration of justice to the nationals of all Members of the United Nations.

The rights conferred by this article on nationals of Members of the United Nations apply equally to companies and associations controlled by such nationals and organized in accordance with the law of any Member of the United Nations.

Article 10

Measures taken to give effect to article 9 of this Agreement shall be subject always to the overriding duty of the Administering Authority in accordance with Article 76 of the United Nations Charter to promote the political, economic, social and educational advancement of the inhabitants of the Territory, to carry out the other basic objectives of the International Trusteeship System, and to maintain peace, order and good government. The Administering Authority shall in particular be free:

(*a*) To organize essential public services and works on such terms and conditions as it thinks just;

(*b*) To create monopolies of a purely fiscal character in order to provide the Territory with the fiscal resources which seem best suited to local requirements, or otherwise to serve the interests of the inhabitants of the Territory;

(*c*) Where the interests of the economic advancement of the inhabitants of the Territory may require it, to establish or permit to be established, for specific purposes, other monopolies or undertakings having in them an element of monopoly, under conditions of proper public control; provided that, in the selection of agencies to carry out the purposes of this paragraph, other than agencies controlled by the Government or those in which the Government participates, the Administering Authority shall not discriminate on grounds of nationality against Members of the United Nations or their nationals.

Article 11

Nothing in this Agreement shall entitle any Member of the United Nations to claim for itself or for its nationals, companies and associations, the benefits of article 9 of this Agreement in any respect in which it does not give to the inhabitants, companies and associations of the Territory equality of treatment with the nationals, companies and associations of the State which it treats most favorably.

Article 12

The Administering Authority shall, as may be appropriate to the circumstances of the Territory, continue and extend a general system of elementary education designed to abolish illiteracy and to facilitate the vocational and cultural advancement of the population, child and adult, and shall similarly provide such facilities as may prove desirable and practicable in the interests of the inhabitants for qualified students to receive secondary and higher education, including professional training.

Article 13

The Administering Authority shall ensure, in the Territory, complete freedom of conscience and, so far as is consistent with the requirements of public order and morality, freedom of religious teaching and the free exercise of all forms of worship. Subject to the provisions of article 8 of this Agreement and the local law, missionaries who are nationals of Members of the United Nations shall be free to enter the Territory and to travel and reside therein, to acquire and possess property, to erect religious buildings and to open schools and hospitals in the Territory. The provisions of this article shall not, however, affect the right and duty

No. 118

of the Administering Authority to exercise such control as he may consider necessary for the maintenance of peace, order and good government and for the educational advancement of the inhabitants of the Territory, and to take all measures required for such control.

Article 14

Subject only to the requirements of public order, the Administering Authority shall guarantee to the inhabitants of the Territory freedom of speech, of the press, of assembly and of petition.

Article 15

The Administering Authority may arrange for the co-operation of the Territory in any regional advisory commission, regional technical organization, or other voluntary association of States, any specialized international bodies, public or private, or other forms of international activity not inconsistent with the United Nations Charter.

Article 16

The Administering Authority shall make to the General Assembly of the United Nations an annual report on the basis of a questionnaire drawn up by the Trusteeship Council in accordance with Article 88 of the United Nations Charter. Such reports shall include information concerning the measures taken to give effect to suggestions and recommendations of the General Assembly and the Trusteeship Council. The Administering Authority shall designate an accredited representative to be present at the sessions of the Trusteeship Council at which the reports of the Administering Authority with regard to the Territory are considered.

Article 17

Nothing in this Agreement shall affect the right of the Administering Authority to propose, at any future date, the amendment of this Agreement for the purpose of designating the whole or part of the Territory as a strategic area or for any other purpose not inconsistent with the basic objectives of the International Trusteeship System.

Article 18

The terms of this Agreement shall not be altered or amended except as provided in Article 79 and Article 83 or 85, as the case may be, of the United Nations Charter.

No. 118

APPENDIX 2

Article 19

If any dispute whatever should arise between the Administering Authority and another Member of the United Nations relating to the interpretation or application of the provisions of this Agreement, such dispute, if it cannot be settled by negotiation or other means, shall be submitted to the International Court of Justice, provided for in Chapter XIV of the United Nations Charter.

1279 (XIII). Hearing of Mr. John Kale

The General Assembly,

Having granted a hearing to Mr. John Kale on the Trust Territory of Ruanda-Urundi,[18]

Draws the attention of the Trusteeship Council to the statement of the petitioner on the Trust Territory of Ruanda-Urundi.

782nd plenary meeting,
5 December 1958.

1280 (XIII). Report of the Trusteeship Council

The General Assembly,

Having examined the report of the Trusteeship Council covering the work of its twenty-first and twenty-second sessions,[19]

1. *Takes note* of the report of the Trusteeship Council;

2. *Recommends* that the Trusteeship Council, in its future deliberations, should take into account the comments and suggestions made during the discussion of its report at the thirteenth session of the General Assembly.

782nd plenary meeting,
5 December 1958.

1281 (XIII). Resumption of the thirteenth session of the General Assembly to consider the question of the future of the Trust Territories of the Cameroons under French administration and the Cameroons under United Kingdom administration

The General Assembly

Decides to resume its thirteenth session on 20 February 1959 to consider exclusively the question of the future of the Trust Territories of the Cameroons under French administration and the Cameroons under United Kingdom administration.

782nd plenary meeting,
5 December 1958.

1282 (XIII). Question of the future of the Trust Territories of the Cameroons under French administration and the Cameroons under United Kingdom administration

The General Assembly,

Having considered the memorandum dated 12 November 1958 of the Government of France[20] concerning the future of the Cameroons under French administration,

Noting the statement made by the representative of the United Kingdom of Great Britain and Northern Ireland[21] to the Fourth Committee on 15 November 1958 concerning the future of the Cameroons under United Kingdom administration,

Noting the statements made by the representative of France, Prime Minister of the Cameroons under French administration, to the Fourth Committee on 11 November 1958[22] and on 14 November 1958[23] and the wishes expressed by the Legislative Assembly of the Cameroons in its resolution of 24 October 1958.

Having heard the petitioners on the conditions in the Trust Territories of the Cameroons under French administration and the Cameroons under United Kingdom administration,[24]

Recalling that a visiting mission of the Trusteeship Council is now in the said Territories, in pursuance of Council resolutions 1907 (XXII) of 28 July 1958 and 1924 (S-IX) of 7 November 1958 adopted by the Council at its twenty-second session and ninth special session, respectively,

1. *Notes* the declarations of the Government of France[20] that the Cameroons under French administration is to achieve independence on 1 January 1960, thus fulfilling the objectives of the Trusteeship System;

2. *Notes* the statement made by the representative of the United Kingdom of Great Britain and Northern Ireland[21] that the Cameroons under United Kingdom administration is expected to achieve in 1960 the objectives set forth in Article 76 b of the Charter of the United Nations;

3. *Requests* the Trusteeship Council to examine, as early as possible during its twenty-third session, the reports of the United Nations Visiting Mission to Trust Territories in West Africa, 1958, and to transmit the same, with its observations and recommendations, to the General Assembly not later than 20 February 1959, to enable the Assembly, in consultation with the Administering Authorities, to take the necessary measures in connexion with the full attainment of the objectives of the Trusteeship System in the two Territories.

782nd plenary meeting,
5 December 1958.

1326 (XIII). Report on social conditions in Non-Self-Governing Territories

The General Assembly,

Recalling that by its resolutions 643 (VII) of 10 December 1952 and 929 (X) of 8 November 1955 it had approved two reports on social conditions prepared by the Committee on Information from Non-Self-Governing Territories in 1952[25] and 1955,[26]

Having received the further report on social conditions prepared in 1958 by the Committee on Information from Non-Self-Governing Territories,[27]

Noting the valuable contributions of the specialized agencies concerned and of the Secretariat,

1. *Approves* the further report on social conditions prepared in 1958 by the Committee on Information from Non-Self-Governing Territories, and considers that it

---

[18] See *Official Records of the General Assembly, Thirteenth Session, Fourth Committee,* 804th and 805th meetings.
[19] *Official Records of the General Assembly, Thirteenth Session, Supplement No. 4* (A/3822).
[20] *Ibid., Thirteenth Session, Annexes,* agenda item 13, document A/C.4/388.
[21] See *Official Records of the General Assembly, Thirteenth Session, Fourth Committee,* 803rd meeting.

[22] *Ibid.,* 794th meeting.
[23] *Ibid.,* 800th meeting.
[24] *Ibid.,* 775th, 776th, 779th, 780th, 792nd, 807th and 808th meetings.
[25] *Official Records of the General Assembly, Seventh Session, Supplement No. 18* (A/2219), part two.
[26] *Ibid., Tenth Session, Supplement No. 16* (A/2908), part two.
[27] *Ibid., Thirteenth Session, Supplement No. 15* (A/3837), part two.

APPENDIX 4

to be constituted in Ruanda-Urundi will give urgent consideration to these problems",[5]

Recalling that the Trusteeship Council and the Committee on Rural Economic Development have in the past made various studies of the problem of population, land utilization and land tenure system in Ruanda-Urundi,

Bearing in mind that the majority of the petitioners are agreed that this problem is of vital importance to the Territory,

Considering that a satisfactory land tenure system is essential to the peaceful evolution and satisfactory economic development of newly independent territories,

1. *Recommends* that the Administering Authority urgently request the United Nations and the specialized agencies, under the technical assistance programmes, to dispatch an expert mission to study the problem of land tenure and land utilization in Ruanda-Urundi, in co-operation with the local authorities, with a view to determining how far the present system is prejudicial to the Territory's social and economic development, and to recommend corrective measures;

2. *Expresses the hope* that the Technical Assistance Board and the specialized agencies concerned will give favourable consideration to such a request.

994th plenary meeting,
21 April 1961.

1607 (XV). Dissemination of information on the United Nations and the International Trusteeship System in Trust Territories

The General Assembly,

Recalling its resolution 1276 (XIII) of 5 December 1958 and resolution 1410 (XIV) of 5 December 1959 whereby the General Assembly, *inter alia,* requested the Secretary-General to initiate discussions with the Administering Authorities of Trust Territories with a view to establishing, during 1960, in at least some of the larger Trust Territories, such as Tanganyika, Ruanda-Urundi and New Guinea, United Nations information centres in which the responsible positions would be occupied preferably by indigenous inhabitants of the Trust Territories concerned,

Having perused the report of the Secretary-General[6] prepared in accordance with General Assembly resolution 1410 (XIV), and observing therefrom that the dissemination of information on the United Nations among the peoples of the Trust Territories is still far from satisfactory,

Keeping in view the special status of Trust Territories and their inhabitants and also the General Assembly's own special responsibilities under Chapters XII and XIII of the Charter of the United Nations,

Reiterating that it is essential, in the General Assembly's view, that the peoples of Trust Territories should receive adequate information concerning the purposes and operation of the United Nations and of the International Trusteeship System, the principles of the Universal Declaration of Human Rights, and the Declaration on the granting of independence to colonial countries and peoples contained in Assembly resolution 1514 (XV) of 14 December 1960,

[5] *Official Records of the General Assembly, Fifteenth Session, Supplement No. 4* (A/4404), part II, chapter II, para. 184.
[6] *Ibid., Fifteenth Session, Annexes,* agenda item 46, documents A/4542 and Add.1.

1. *Takes note* of the report of the Secretary-General on dissemination of information on the United Nations and the International Trusteeship System in Trust Territories;

2. *Considers* that United Nations information centres constitute one of the most important means of disseminating information about the United Nations in these Territories;

3. *Takes note* of the statement of the representative of the United Kingdom of Great Britain and Northern Ireland that, as a result of discussions between the Secretary-General and the Administering Authority, steps have been taken to establish, in the near future, a United Nations information centre in Tanganyika;

4. *Takes further note* of the recommendation in paragraph 224 of the interim report of the United Nations Commission for Ruanda-Urundi[a] that a United Nations information centre should be set up with all possible speed in Ruanda-Urundi;

5. *Requests* the Secretary-General to take the necessary action to establish, without any further delay, in Tanganyika, Ruanda-Urundi and New Guinea, United Nations information centres in which the responsible positions would be occupied by indigenous inhabitants of the Trust Territories concerned;

6. *Invites* the Administering Authorities to extend their co-operation and assistance to the Secretary-General in implementing the present resolution;

7. *Requests* the Secretary-General to ensure the immediate and mass publication and the widest possible circulation and dissemination, in all the Trust Territories through all media of mass communication, of the Declaration on the granting of independence to colonial countries and peoples;

8. *Requests* that the information referred to in the present resolution should be disseminated in the principal local languages as well as in the language of the Administering Authority;

9. *Further requests* the Secretary-General to prepare for the Trusteeship Council at its twenty-seventh session and for the General Assembly at its sixteenth session a report on the implementation of the present resolution.

994th plenary meeting,
21 April 1961.

1608 (XV). The future of the Trust Territory of the Cameroons under United Kingdom administration

The General Assembly,

Recalling its resolution 1350 (XIII) of 13 March 1959 concerning the future of the Trust Territory of the Cameroons under United Kingdom administration in which the General Assembly recommended, *inter alia,* that the Administering Authority take steps, in consultation with the United Nations Plebiscite Commissioner for the Cameroons under United Kingdom Administration, to organize, under the supervision of the United Nations, separate plebiscites in the northern and southern parts of the Cameroons under United Kingdom administration, in order to ascertain the wishes of the inhabitants of the Territory concerning their future, and that the plebiscite in the Northern Cameroons be held about the middle of November 1959

APPENDIX 4

on the basis of the two questions set out in paragraph 2 of the said resolution,

Recalling its resolution 1352 (XIV) of 16 October 1959 whereby it decided, *inter alia*, that a plebiscite in the Southern Cameroons would be held between 30 September 1960 and March 1961, on the basis of the two questions set forth in paragraph 2 of the said resolution,

Recalling further its resolution 1473 (XIV) of 12 December 1959 in which the General Assembly, having considered the results of the plebiscite in the northern part of the Cameroons under United Kingdom administration, recommended the organization by the Administering Authority, in consultation with the United Nations Plebiscite Commissioner, of a further plebiscite to be held in the Northern Cameroons under United Nations supervision between 30 September 1960 and March 1961, on the basis of the two questions defined in paragraph 3 of the said resolution,

Having examined the report of the United Nations Plebiscite Commissioner concerning the two plebiscites held in the Northern and the Southern Cameroons in February 1961[7] and the report of the Trusteeship Council thereon,[8]

Having heard the petitioners,

1. *Expresses its high appreciation* of the work of United Nations Plebiscite Commissioner for the Cameroons under United Kingdom Administration and his staff;

2. *Endorses* the results of the plebiscites that:

(a) The people of the Northern Cameroons have, by a substantial majority, decided to achieve independence by joining the independent Federation of Nigeria;

(b) The people of the Southern Cameroons have similarly decided to achieve independence by joining the independent Republic of Cameroun;

3. *Considers that*, the people of the two parts of the Trust Territory having freely and secretly expressed their wishes with regard to their respective futures in accordance with General Assembly resolutions 1352 (XIV) and 1473 (XIV), the decisions made by them through democratic processes under the supervision of the United Nations should be immediately implemented;

4. *Decides* that, the plebiscites having been taken separately with differing results, the Trusteeship Agreement of 13 December 1946 concerning the Cameroons under United Kingdom administration shall be terminated, in accordance with Article 76 b of the Charter of the United Nations and in agreement with the Administering Authority, in the following manner:

(a) With respect to the Northern Cameroons, on 1 June 1961, upon its joining the Federation of Nigeria as a separate province of the Northern Region of Nigeria;

(b) With respect to the Southern Cameroons, on 1 October 1961, upon its joining the Republic of Cameroun;

5. *Invites* the Administering Authority, the Government of the Southern Cameroons and the Republic of Cameroun to initiate urgent discussions with a view to finalizing, before 1 October 1961, the arrangements by which the agreed and declared policies of the parties concerned will be implemented.

994th plenary meeting,
21 April 1961.

---

[7] *Ibid.*, agenda item 13, addendum, document A/4727.
[8] *Ibid.*, agenda item 13, document A/4726.

1609 (XV). The future of Tanganyika

The General Assembly,

Having considered the communication of 17 April 1961 from the Administering Authority,[9]

1. *Notes* that the Governments of the United Kingdom of Great Britain and Northern Ireland and of Tanganyika have agreed that Tanganyika should become independent on 28 December 1961;

2. *Resolves,* in agreement with the Administering Authority, that the Trusteeship Agreement for Tanganyika, approved by the General Assembly on 13 December 1946, shall cease to be in force upon the accession of Tanganyika to independence on 28 December 1961;

3. *Recommends* that, upon the attainment of its independence on 28 December 1961, Tanganyika shall be admitted to membership in the United Nations in accordance with Article 4 of the Charter of the United Nations;

4. *Requests* the Administering Authority to present to the Trusteeship Council, at its twenty-seventh session to be held in the summer of 1961, further information on the constitutional conference held at Dar es Salaam in March 1961 and on the measures already taken or planned by the Administering Authority to ensure the transfer of powers to the legislative and executive organs of Tanganyika.

995th plenary meeting,
21 April 1961.

1610 (XV). Report of the Trusteeship Council

The General Assembly,

Having received the report of the Trusteeship Council covering the period from 7 August 1959 to 30 June 1960,[10]

1. *Takes note* of the report of the Trusteeship Council;

2. *Recommends* that the Administering Authorities take account of the recommendations and observations contained in the report.

995th plenary meeting,
21 April 1961.

1611 (XV). Offers by Member States of study and training facilities for inhabitants of Trust Territories

The General Assembly,

Recalling its resolution 1411 (XIV) of 5 December 1959, which requested the Secretary-General to prepare, for the fifteenth session of the General Assembly, a report on the actual use of scholarships and training facilities offered by Member States to students from Trust Territories, in accordance with its resolution 557 (VI) of 18 January 1952 which invited Member States to make scholarships available to qualified students from Trust Territories,

1. *Takes note* of the report of the Secretary-General[11] and of part I, chapter VI, section D, of the report of the Trusteeship Council,[10] containing information on

---

[9] *Ibid.*, document A/C.4/489.
[10] *Ibid., Fifteenth Session, Supplement No. 4* (A/4404).
[11] *Ibid., Fifteenth Session, Annexes,* agenda item 47, documents A/4498 and Add.1.

www.ingramcontent.com/pod-product-compliance
Lightning Source LLC
Chambersburg PA
CBHW020708270326
41928CB00005B/325